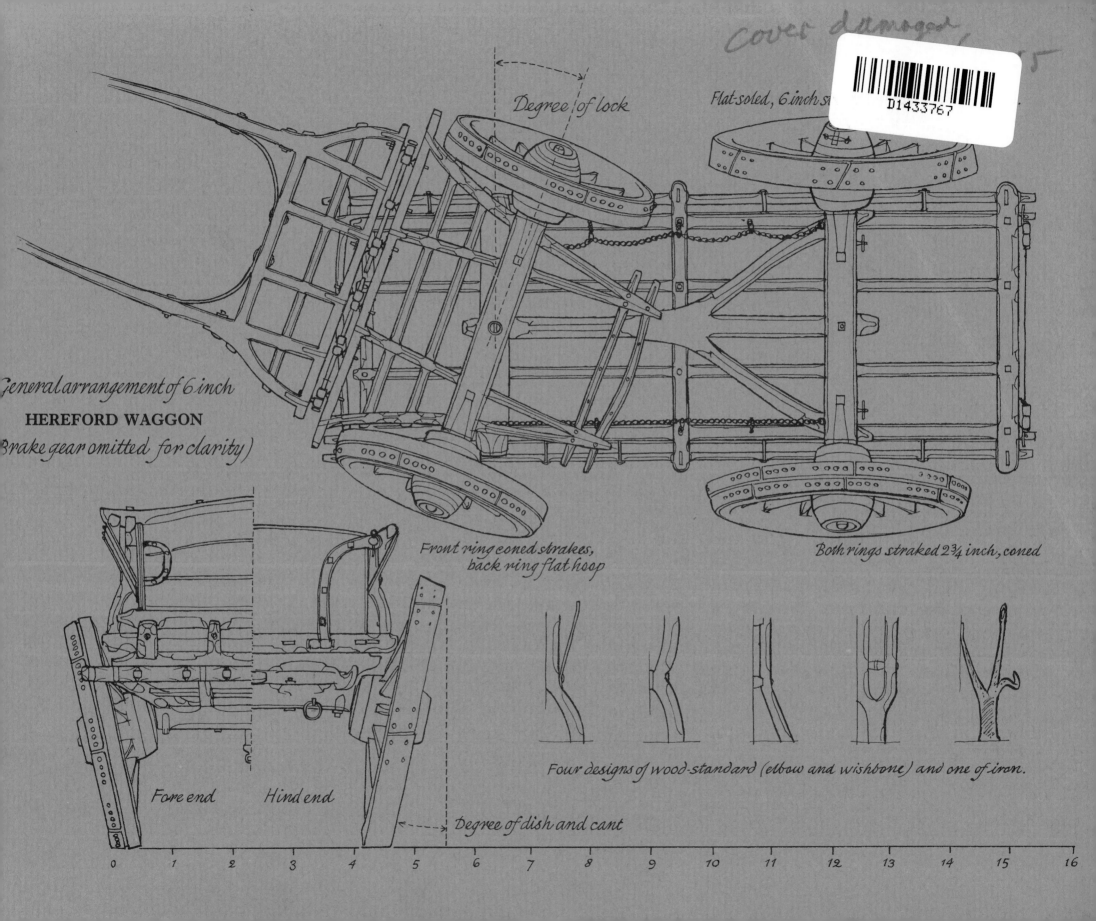

Degree of lock

Flat-soled, 6 inch s...

General arrangement of 6 inch

HEREFORD WAGGON

(Brake gear omitted for clarity)

Front ring coned strakes,
back ring flat hoop

Both rings straked 2¾ inch, coned

Fore end   Hind end

Degree of dish and cant

Four designs of wood-standard (elbow and wishbone) and one of iron.

0   1   2   3   4   5   6   7   8   9   10   11   12   13   14   15   16

THE FARM WAGGONS
of England and Wales

THE FARM WAGGONS
of England and Wales

JAMES ARNOLD

With twenty-four full-colour plates and a number of drawings

JOHN BAKER

First published 1969
Reprinted with corrections 1974

John Baker (Publishers) Ltd
4, 5 & 6 Soho Square, London W1V 6AD

© *James Arnold* 1969

This book has been set in Imprint 12/13 *pt*
Reproduced and printed by offset lithography in Great Britain by
Hollen Street Press Ltd, Slough, Buckinghamshire.
ISBN 0 212 99839 0

CONTENTS

PREFACE

During the nineteenth century the wheelwrights of England and Wales produced about a hundred different designs of farm-waggon. This total includes all four-wheeled waggons, but is exclusive of drays, spring-carts, miller's waggons and every design of two-wheeled vehicle.

These waggons have come to be accepted as traditional to each county or region. In some counties, there were but one or two designs, while in others there were more. The twenty-four plates, in full colour, are intended to give an indication of their range and to spread the net as widely as possible, geographically.

This work is a description of waggons, and is based both on personal investigation 'in the field' and on enquiry and research among the various sources of information. The making of waggons is not described, firstly, because the author is not a wheelwright and, secondly, because he has no intention of obtruding himself where a book has already been written, describing the whole matter from the standing tree to the finished product with a feeling that is intensely moving and which will never be surpassed. That book, *The Wheelwrights' Shop* by George Sturt and published by Cambridge University Press, will be mentioned several times. Likewise the history of waggons, from the primitive conveyance onward, is not included, because this has been covered by Geraint Jenkins in *The English Farm Wagon*, published by David and Charles and in *Agricultural Transport in Wales*, published by The National Museum of Wales.

This work may be described as a summary of 25 years of study and research, all made in the course of many miles of cycling. Even after the war waggons were still fairly abundant. Some were found in unexpected places and while many were still in use, others were 'so far gone' as to present no more than a valuable clue. The drawings have been prepared from a great many field sketches. A great deal of research has been made in the time and will continue to be made, for the subject is virtually inexhaustible. The author will always be profoundly grateful for information, the loan of photos, old lists, etc. What might be considered no more than trivial can well prove to be of the utmost value. One of the author's most prized possessions is a letter from a retired blacksmith, now in his 80's, written in a meticulous hand.

INTRODUCTION

In the older way of arable farming, the way which had evolved as the still older open fields were enclosed, the four wheeled farm-waggon had a vital place, which it held until it was eventually ousted by the requirements of fully mechanised farming of the present day.

These waggons had always been so well constructed that it was not unusual to expect them to last for a hundred years. In good hands they could exceed that time, but too often they suffered excessive wear and tear and indifferent ownership. Such longevity became an anachronism in the modern economy, where permanence is not a good thing. There is now neither time nor use for it. The harvest festival has declined to a mere formality, without spiritual impetus. The last sheaf of corn, the corn-maiden, the dollies, the last waggon-load and the procession shouting to proclaim to the nearest farms that all was safely in, then finally, the Harvest Home. All was a climax to the farming year and for better or for worse, sentiment decreed that the waggons and their horses should be the resplendent centre piece.

Farming is different now. Nature is no longer the collaborator, to be propitiated and thanked, but is the enemy, to be eliminated where possible, or otherwise be kept in its place. In any case, the tractor, the combine and the baler somehow do not lend themselves to decoration nor do they stimulate the festive occasion.

The four-wheeled waggon was never in universal use in every county. Generally, it was a vehicle of the lowland farms, although exceptionally it was to be found on certain types of terrain which one would have considered too hilly.

It we take a map of England and Wales and, starting on the East Coast at about Whitby, carry this line across the Vale of York to the North Midlands, near Derby and the mouth of the River Dee, then down through the Marches to the Vale of Glamorgan, we may say that the waggon was in common use in every county south and east of this demarcation and from Trevose Head to the North Foreland. From the Marches, there were a number of penetrations into Wales. North and West of the demarcation and including Ireland and Scotland, waggons gave place to various types of two-wheeled cart, and sled.

Within this Waggon Zone, every county had one or more designs of waggon, not always native in origin. Exclusive of variations on each of the main designs, the total must have been in the region of a hundred, with the greatest number occurring in East Anglia and between Swindon, Bristol and Shrewsbury.

According to the *Oxford English Dictionary*, a waggon (with double or single g) is 'a strong, four-wheeled vehicle designed for the transport of heavy goods', or 'an open four-wheeled vehicle, built for carrying hay, corn etc., consisting of a long body furnished with shelboards. 1573'. The first recorded uses of words may here be mentioned: Wain, OE. Tumbril, 1440. Cart, 1602. Trolley, 1823. Spring-cart, 1823.

The waggon, though more lightly built than the kind which was designed expressly for road-transport, was nevertheless in most cases a cumbersome vehicle. If we read the works of the eighteenth century writers, we find that the harvest-waggon had changed very little and that problems of draught were besetting wheelwrights without any satisfactory solution being achieved. The four-wheeler had a great capacity, although many, when fully laden, became unwieldy and required considerable room in which to turn round. The two-wheeled cart and the tumbril were far more manageable and the capacity of the largest of these was not less than half that of a waggon. They could also be turned much more easily, and were indispensable on the more hilly farms and for winter work everywhere.

In the East Midlands, many two-wheeled carts were adapted to be coupled to the fore-carriage taken from an old waggon, with the addition of a framework to support a large, horizontal ladder, which extended well forward over the shafts. It was called a Hermaphrodite, or more commonly, among farmers, a 'mufferer'. The Trolley came into use earlier than the dictionary suggests, at least by the end of the eighteenth century. Most trolleys had an undercarriage, similar to the waggon, on which was fitted a large open framework to carry the harvest load, so that they were unsuitable for transporting root crops etc. The trolley found favour and became numerous throughout the West Midlands. For lighter transport, some four-wheelers were fitted with elliptic springs, to be known as Spring-carts, but they were unsuitable for use on farm-land. The tumbril or tip-cart, had a body hinged underneath and held by a locking device which released the body so as to tip up and discharge its load.

The mountain and moorland farms, generally situated above the 1,000 foot contour, have always produced a relatively light crop of hay or corn. For the transport of this, a light cart has always been adequate. In Wales, one still sees the handy little Gambo. It has a low-level floor, with short side rails, or stiles, sufficient to keep the load clear of the wheels. Wherever the use of the Gambo or its equivalent, was impracticable on the steeper hill-sides, then various kinds of sled were, and still are used. They are common on many Scottish lowland farms, where the hay is stooked on tripods, which are loaded complete on to sleds or long-carts. In central Wales and western Shropshire, they used a curious hybrid, a substantially constructed long-sled fitted with large wheels. It was nose-heavy, which meant that it always ran on the front sled and its wheels.

In the southern counties of England, many farmers used a long low cart, sometimes known as a Wain or Harvest Cart, but to confuse matters, often referred to as a Scotch Cart. It bore some resemblance to the Gambo, and had a low floor and shallow sides which were gently arched over the two wheels. Such carts were noted at Kelmscott, near Lechlade, at Terling, in Essex, and near Henley-on-Thames. They were also produced in large numbers by the Bristol Wagon and Carriage Works, who called them Harvest Carts, to carry 30 cwt.

During the nineteenth century, waggons mostly continued to be complex in structure, but toward the end there was a definite move toward simpler construction. This was due to economic causes. Mass production could only be accomplished by dispensing with the traditional way of manufacture, the ornament and decoration. Now, in retrospection, we realise that those somewhat austere waggons were by no means lacking in beauty.

There were two main designs. One was known as the Boat Waggon and the second as the Barge, because of some resemblance to those craft. The Boat was more or less standardised, but the Barge waggons appeared in considerable variety. At first, both designs retained the tongue-pole, but the later ones dispensed with it, enabling the waggons, which had small fore-wheels, to be fully-locking.

Crook, bed-bearer, side, main-side, sole, blade . . . not as one might think, the names of different parts of a waggon, but different names for the same part, and a hint of the great variety of all the names. Even a name might be variously spelled . . . cleat, clete, clout.

The absence of a universal terminology created no difficulties since the business of wheelwrighting was very much parish-bound. It mattered nothing that a Lincolnshire man spoke of a 'shore-stake', while the equivalent part of a Hereford waggon was an 'elbow', or that the Hereford man knew a 'slote' and a Cotswold man a 'corner-bar'. When, however, one is writing about waggons collectively, one is straightaway confronted with the problem of common reference. While some part-names are self-explanatory, this is far from the case with others. So the writer has exercised himself fairly loosely all through the text. To use exclusively, the names known in one county, might suggest a bias. For this reason, the table of part-names and keyed diagrams have been placed very early in the book.

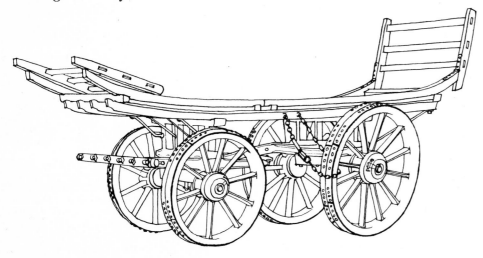

A Trolley, with hinged ends, noted in 1974 at Aymestrey, near Wigmore, Herefordshire. Early 19th century. Blue frames. Red undercarriage.

A Hermaphrodite waggon, noted in 1949, near Shipston-on-Stour, Warwickshire. Yellow body. Red undercarriage and frames.

STRUCTURE AND EQUIPMENT

THE UNDERCARRIAGE

This consisted of a hind- and fore-carriage, to which latter the shafts were joined. The two carriages, which carried the wheels, were joined by a central pole which was rigidly braced to the hind-carriage, but loosely secured to the fore-carriage, permitting free swivelling.

The hind-carriage consisted of an axle-bed, to which the wheels were attached and above it a bolster on which the body rested. The pole and its braces were secured by bolts between the bed and the bolster.

The fore-carriage was more complex and consisted of an axle-bed and a bolster, between which a lateral framework was secured. It was to the front of this frame that the shafts were hinged. This carriage rotated freely on a central pin, under a pillow, which was part of the body. The meeting surfaces of bolster and pillow were very slightly convex, to give a freer movement than would be obtainable with two flat surfaces, and also to provide lateral stability over uneven ground. The central pin was very long, and passed right through the pillow, bolster, pole and bed, beneath which it was secured with a split-pin called a feather.

The fore-carriage frame consisted of two or four members arranged fore-and-aft, sometimes parallel and sometimes splayed outward toward the front, where they were braced by transverse pieces called keys. The fore-and-aft members were often called hounds and their tail ends' carried a transverse piece, called a slider which braced them and bore continuously against the underside of the pole.

This arrangement had evolved quite early in the history of the waggon, and lasted until the advent of the fully-locking type. In the new arrangement, the hind- and fore-carriages were separate units, each being permanently attached to the body and braced with iron rods. Stability was obtained by fitting two large flat iron rings to the pillow and the bolster, so that in continuous bearing, they turned against each other.

The early waggons had their axle-beds and arms in one piece, called an axle-tree. This was quite massive, about six inches square and usually about six feet in length. Only the best beech, which had been seasoned iron hard, was used, and very great skill was required in the setting-out and the making. Some of the wooden-axled waggons may occasionally be seen, and a close-examination of these centenarians will show the thicker arms.

By the second quarter of the nineteenth century, many waggons were being built with the beds and arms in separate parts, bolted together.

The beds were now of elm and the arms of case-hardened steel, supplied ready for fitment, from Birmingham. In both the older type and the new, the arms taper from the back toward the point, and there was a corresponding taper inside the nave of the wheel. An iron cleat was fitted to the under bearing surface of the wooden arm, which provided a wood to iron bearing. When the iron axle was introduced, a cast iron wheel-box was inserted inside the wooden nave. There was much head shaking at the time, since there were points in favour of either wood or steel arms. Some maintained that the wooden arms 'ran' better. The five-inch maximum diameter of the wooden arms no doubt contributed. The new type of bed, however, was easier to make and all together, was said to weigh less.

The passing of the old axle-tree was a 'knock on the door', a portent of other changes yet to come. The wooden axle belonged to a time more permanent than we of today can comprehend, a time when 'things always had been so'.

There were two methods of joining the shafts to the **fore**-carriage. By the first, the two butt-ends of the shafts overlapped the fore-ends of the hounds and were secured to them by a single iron draught-pin which ran right through from one side to the other, usually the nearside, where it was held by a washer and split-pin. By the second method, a long transverse bar of wood was morticed to the front of the hounds and a corresponding bar to the shafts. Each carried a set of barrel-eye hinges through which a draught pin was run. While only one pair of shafts could be attached by the first method, the second permitted either one or two pairs to be attached. The fore-carriage splinter-bar could be as much as six feet long, so there was room enough for double-shafts, side by side.

Each shaft blade was of ash, joined near the butt by a system of cross-pieces which had tenoned ends protruding through the blades. The whole arrangement was braced by two iron bars variously shaped according to county practice. Some distance from the toes of the blades, a set of iron loops or staples was fitted, to which the harness chains were coupled.

The arrangement of the components of the fore-carriage depended upon the method of shaft attachment. When this was done by draught-pin alone, then very often there were only two hounds, though some wheelwrights preferred four. But four were always used when splinter-

	KENT F. Heathfield Ashford	SUSSEX G. Weller Sompting	SURREY G. Sturt Farnham	COTSWOLDS G. Swainston Stow-on-the-Wold	BANBURY F. Sumner Cropredy	GLOUCESTER W. H. J. Drew Frampton Cotterell	HEREFORD N. Wheeler Fownhope	HERTFORD G. W. Casbon Barley	NORTHAMPTON L. W. Phillips Flore	HOLLAND J. P. Bingham Long Sutton
1	Sole	Crook	Sidepiece	Crook	Front crook	Blade	Bedpiece	Side	Main Side	Sole
2	Hindsole	Side		Side	Hind Side				Short Side	
3	Cap Piece	Front Dware	Fore Shutlock	Nosepiece	Nosepiece	Under Head	Front Cross ledge	Forebridge	Nosepiece	Dress Piece
4	Middle Dware	Middle Dware	Main Beam	Crossledge	Middle Crossbed	Middle Bridge	Middlebed Piece	Crossbar	Middle Crossbridge	Middle Cross Bearer
5	Hind Dware	Hind Dware	Hind Shutlock	Spreader Piece	Hind Crossbed	Tail Bridge	Back Cross ledge	Hind Bridge	Hind Crossbridge	Hindbuck
6	Middle Sole	Summer	Summer	Runner	Runner	Summer	Summer Rail	Summer	Middle Piece	Middlefill or Sole
7	Panel Board	Panel Board	Panel Board	Side Board	Side Board	Side Board	Side Board	Side Board	Side Panel	Panel Board
8	Panel Board	Front Panel Board	Head Board	Front Board	Front Board	Head Name Board	Front Board	Front Board	Front Board	Front Board
9	Hind Hawk	Tail Bd. or Hawk	Tail Board	Arch	Tail Board	Tail Board	Tail Board	Tale Board	Tail Board	Tail Board
10	Lade	Top Body Lade	Top Rave	Long Rath	Rave Rail	Rave	Bed Rave	Main Rave	Top Rail	Top Runner
11	Middle Lade	Middle Lade	Middle Rave			Dripple	Middle Bed Rave	Middle Rave	Body Rail	Middle Runner
12	Ladeboard	Outside Lade	Out Rave	Wheel Bow	Wheel Bow	Hoop & Horn	Barge Rave	Top Rave	Rave Rail	Outside Runner
13	Front Hawk	Bridle	Head Piece		Forebuck	Head	Front Bull Rave		Forebuck	Front Top-piece
14		Clip	Running Pin	Corner Bar	Side Iron	Head Stave	Slote			
15	Shore Stave	Shore Staff/N. Iron	Staff	Standard		Strouts/Spur Iron	Elbow	False Stuck	Crutch	Shore Stake
16	Crook	Strouter	Strouter		Standard	Strout	Full Standard		Crutch	
17	Stave	Staff	Stretcher		Spar	Flat		Side Standard	Stave	Spindle
18		Shore Stay	Stay		Rave Iron	Y Stay	Side Stay		Rave Iron	Stay
19	Axle Bed	Axle Bed	Exbed		Bed	Axle Case	Axle Bed	Bed	Axle Bed	Axle Bed
20	Arm	Arm	Arm	Arm	Arm	Grease Axle	Axle	Arm	Arm	Axle Arm
21	Carriage Bolster	Bottom Pillow	Bolster		Bottom Bolster	Carriage Bolster	Guide Bolster	Bottom Bolster	Bolster	Carriage Bolster
22	Top Bolster	Top Pillow	Pillow		Top Bolster	Body Bolster	Bed Bolster	Top Bolster	Body Bolster	Top Bolster
23	Swimmer Pole	Waggon Pole	Tongue Pole	Tun Pole	Tail Pole	Centre Pole	Carriage Pole	Tongue Pole	Tail Pole	Carriage Pole
24		Brace	Spreader	Wing	Spreader	Side Stay	Hip	Tongue	Tail Brace	Side Shear
25		Perch Bolt	Round Pin		Master Pin	Main Pin	Dropper Pin	Perch Bolt	Master Pin	Carriage Bolt
26	Hound	Hound	Hound		Guide	Carriage Blade	Guide	Guide	Main Guide	Carriage Shear
27	Bridge Bar	Slider	Sweep	Slider	Slider	Slide Bar	Slider	Slide Bar	Slide	Brigtree
28	Rod Pin	Draught Bar	Limmer Bolt		Shaft Bar	Shaft Pin	Guidehead*	Shaft Pin	Draught Pin	Shaft Bolt*
29	Shutter	Rod Key	Bolt	Shuth	Shuttle	Shaft Bar	Cross Piece	Shickle Bar	Shaft Bar	Slat
30	Rod	Rod	Sharp	Sharve	Sharp	Shaft	Shaft	Shaft	Shaft	Shaft
31	Nave	Nave	Stock	Stock	Hub	Nave or Stock	Stock	Nave	Hub	Nave
32	Spoke	Spoke	Spoke	Spoke	Spoke	Spoke	Spoke	Spoke	Spoke	Spoke
33	Felloe	Felloe	Felloe	Felloe	Felloe	Felloe	Felloe	Felloe	Felloe	Felloe
34	Tyre	Tyre/Strake	Tyre/Strake	Tyre/Strake	Tyre/Strake	Tyre/Strake	Tyre/Strake	Tyre/Strake	Tyre/Strake	Tyre
35	Bond	Nave Bond	Bond	Bond	Bond	Stock Hoop	Bond	Nave Hoop	Bond	Nave Hoop
36	Linch Pin	Linch Pin	Linch Pin	Linch Pin	Linch Pin	Linch Pin	Linch Pin	Linch Pin	Linch Pin	Axle Pin
37	Pole	Harvest Pole	Ladder	Gate	Ladder	Ladder	Thripples	Ladder	Ladder	High Raves
							*Splinter-bar			*Splinter-bar

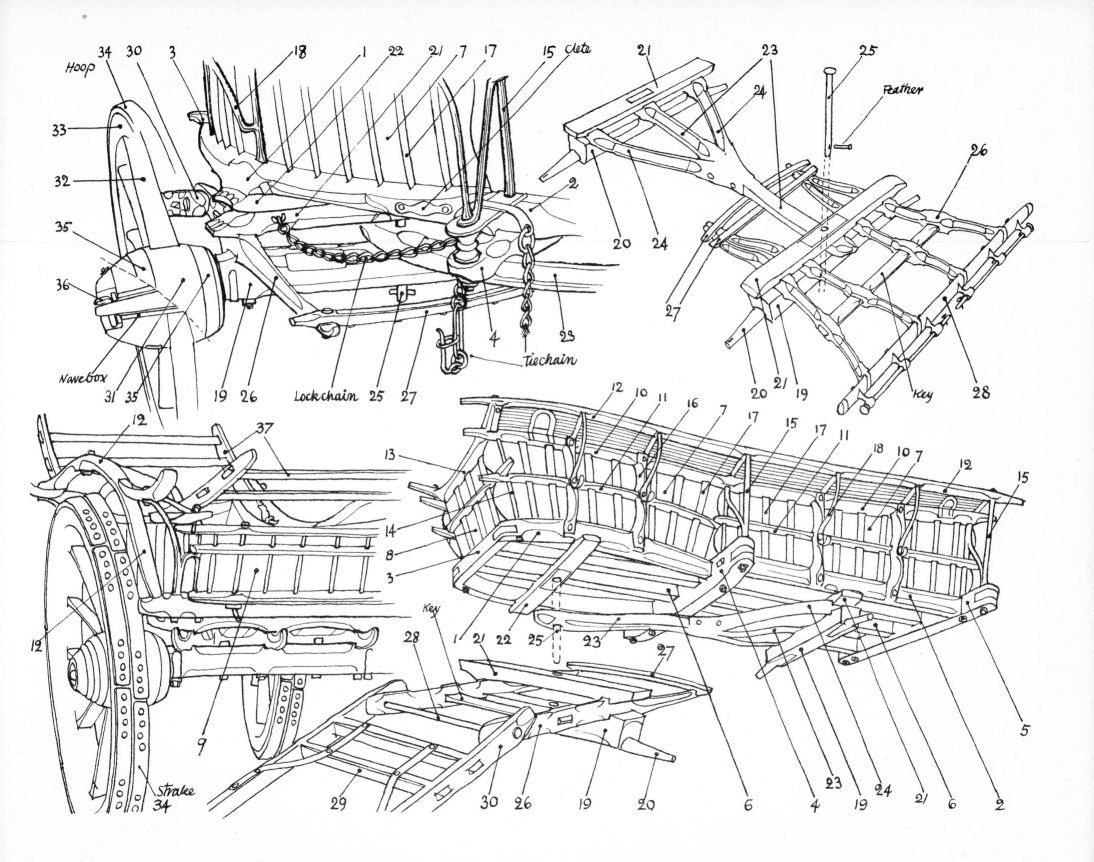

Hoop

34   30   3   18   1   22   21   7   17   15   Clete   21   23   25   Feather

33

32

35   2

36   26

4   23

Navebox   19   26   Lockchain   25   27   Tiechain   20   24   27   20   21   19   Key   28

31   35

12   37

13   12   10   11   16   7   17   15   17   11   18   10   7   12   15

14

8

3

12   9   Key   28   1   21   22   25   23   27   6   4   23   19   24   21   6   2

Strake
34   29   30   26   19   20

bars were incorporated. By splaying the outside pair of hounds so that they just cleared the wheels, four widely spaced points of attachment were obtained. By fitting six or eight barrel-eye hinges, alternative positions for single or double shafts were provided. In addition to many of the traditional waggons, all trollies and spring-carts had the splinter-bar attachment.

Draught-pins were usually, but not invariably, inserted from the offside. A few photos show the opposite fitting. Some waggons had hounds so short in front that the pin had to be inserted between the wheel-spokes, but most waggons had hounds long enough for the pin to be clear of the wheels. If a pin got bent it would not go through and it was a blacksmith's job to get it straight again. In nearly every county, the shaft butts were outside the hounds, but a few wheelwrights such as Gerring, of Milton, Berkshire; Horder, of Loxwood, Sussex; and Blank, of Bradwell, Essex, set their shafts between the hounds. Double shafts each had their separate pins, inserted from the outside and secured in the centre.

In nearly every design of waggon, the slider on the rear of the fore-carriage was lap-joined to the hounds and above them, and secured by bolts, but in a few cases, it was morticed to the hounds and reinforced with cleats. This was practised by Thomas Workman, of Wotton-under-Edge, Glos., and by Blank, of Bradwell, Essex. Some makers, such as those of West Shropshire and Herefordshire fitted their sliders to a four-hound carriage.

Wheelwrights were not at all afraid of plenty of curves in their waggons and were most careful in the selection of suitable timber. This was particularly important in regard to the shafts for which the grain must 'follow through'. Equally, it was important for the curved side frames of the body. Timber would be noted in the forest, selected and put by for some part of the waggon.

THE WHEELS

The nave of a wheel was invariably made of one piece of elm, because this was the only wood capable of withstanding the morticing of ten to fourteen holes for the spokes as well as the large hole through the centre, for the axle. Only elm, which has a twisting grain, could withstand all the spokes being knocked in, and the subsequent years of use, without splitting or splintering.

The naves were bulging in section, from front to back but were flat for a depth of about four inches at the maximum diameter, where the spokes entered. The forward taper was greater than the rearward. Each spoke-hole was rectangular and went in as far as the axle-hole. At the back of the nave, an iron hoop was shrunk on, and a similar but broader hoop was likewise shrunk on, just in front of the spokes. At the front, called the nose, a slot was cut, to allow a linch-pin to be inserted in the arm after the wheel had been hung, or put on. This slot was closed with a stopper which was secured by a clasp.

The spokes were always made of cleft oak, with the heart of the wood at the back, where the greatest strain was imposed. The rim of a wheel was composed of a ring of felloes, or segments, one to every two spokes. Some builders chose elm for spokes but the great majority preferred oak. When the felloes were put on every two spokes had to be drawn together so that the holes in the backs—the insides—came in line with the tongues, or extremities of the spokes. It has been stated in the Preface that the making of waggons would not be described, but even so, one cannot just pass on without realising why the men who made waggons were called wheelwrights. Herein lay the heart of a remarkable craft. A man might get away with a body slightly askew, but not the wheels.

The sectional shape of the felloes varied according to the width of tread. Most wheels—under four inch tread—had the bellies or inner side and the soles, or outer sides parallel, while the outer face and the inner converged slightly from belly to sole. For wheels with treads of more than three inches soles tapered—see under Dish and Cant. The depth of felloe, about four inches, was necessary to obtain the required strength. Broad wheels, of five or six inch treads, had rather shallow felloes. This produced a rectangle which after chamfering became a D (on its side), not a semi-circle. Some broad felloes had a flat taper on the belly, being deeper at the back. Broad wheels had their spokes nearer the back of the ring than the front.

The main problems of waggon design centred on the wheels. The early vehicles, especially those for road transport, had comparatively large wheels, with little difference between front and back. A large wheel of any kind will certainly roll better than a small one, but there were two difficulties which the wheelwrights sought to overcome. Too large a pair of hind-wheels set the floor so high as to render loading and off-loading difficult. Too large a pair of fore-wheels imposed too much restriction on the turning capacity or wheel-lock. Conversely, if the wheels were too small, then the draught of the vehicle was made unnecessarily heavy. Consider two examples, the large wheeled Oxford waggon and the small wheeled dray and see for yourself which is the easier to manœuvre. One man can move an Oxford, but it will require the urgings of three or four to shift a dray. Somewhere between the extremes of the old road waggon and the dray, there was a happy medium and one has only to consider the astonishing variation in wheel diameters to wonder just where that medium lay.

Wrights were accustomed to term their waggons 'narrow wheeled' or 'broad', according to the width of the wheels—or the tread as they called it. Narrow wheels were no more than four inches across, and broad ones were over four, while the most common widths were from two and a half to three inches. Nearly all broad wheels had six inch treads which were shod with two rings of strakes, but if they were five inches or less, then they were tyred with hoops equal to the tread.

In some regions, notably west of the Severn and about its estuary, the practice of straking wheels continued until the last waggon was built, while in other regions hoop tyres were adopted very early in the nineteenth century. In some counties, broad wheels disappeared very early while in others, they were still being made in this century. While the narrow hooped tyre ran well enough on the lighter soil, many wrights claimed that broad, straked wheels held better on wet, heavy land in hilly country. Between these extremes, the builders in Sussex and Kent latterly made nearly every waggon with four inch or three and a half inch hooped wheels.

It was always the practice to set the spokes a few degrees out of right angles to the axle-line, to produce a flatly coned or dished wheel. The theory that a wheel so built was stronger and more resistant to thrust was contended and disputed without conclusion. Theory and Practice were never resolved and wrights went on very much as their forefathers had done. In one region, wheels were deeply dished, in another only slightly. Whatever the degree of dish and cant, it was imperative that as a wheel rotated, each spoke in turn, at the bottom point of rotation should be vertical at that moment. Each spoke, in turn at the top point of rotation would have an angle to the ground twice that of the degree of dish—see the diagram.

In order that the vertical line be obtained it was necessary to set the

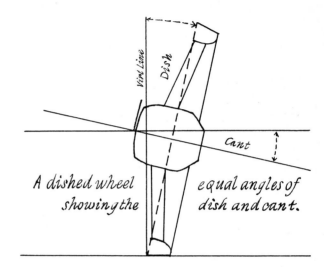

A dished wheel showing the *equal angles of dish and cant.*

arm of the axle pointing down from the horizontal at the corresponding angle. The side thrusts which took place in a moving waggon were set up by the gait of the horse which caused these alternating thrusts. The wheels were continuously running off and back on their axles. As one 'ran off' the opposite 'ran back'. This could be partially counteracted by setting the arms to point a degree or so forward of the true line as well as down. This setting was known as foreway. As in so many things, wrights worked by precedent and something like an innate capacity. The wheels were actually about a quarter of an inch out of line, so that they were pigeon-toed. This could not be detected in a 50 or 60 inch wheel, but it was enough to throw the wear off the extremities of the arms. The alternating click-clack of the moving waggon was one of the little sounds which went with the jingle of the harness.

The common angle of dish and cant was repeated on the sole or periphery of wheels having treads wider than three inches. Treads of less than three inches were too narrow to require coning as it was called. In theory, they ran on their outside edges, but in fact, road and field surface were sufficiently uneven that this could be ignored. The broad wheels, however, were wide enough that they had to be coned.

Most broad wheels were shod with two rings of strakes, each $2\frac{3}{4}$ inches wide, with a half-inch gap between the rings. The dish and cant varied and likewise the coning, or flueing. Some wheels had both rings coned equally, while others had the inner ring flat, that is, without the cone, and this produced a slightly domed tread. A number of Gloucestershire wheelwrights made their wheels this way and some put a hoop in place of the back ring of strakes. William Drew, of Frampton Cotterell, writes—'one reason for the complete tyre on the back was to obtain a flat bearing on the hard road. The strakes being cambered (coned) made a round bearing that would not cut the turf on grass-land. Another reason was that the tyre on the back of the wheel had a direct bearing on the shoulders of the spokes, pulling the wheel together when shrunk on hot, while the strakes would give a little on the front, where the spokes had no shoulders'.

The strakes were always a fraction shorter than the felloes, and over-lapped them so that their joints came almost half-way between the felloe-joints. Not quite, because the two rings were staggered by about two inches, so that they did not fall opposite. This gave better results, because each ring supported the other.

Mr. O. Johnson, of Gorsley-Linton, Herefordshire, now in his 80's, tells me that when he was blacksmith to Teague, of Tibberton, all their wheels were flued in front and flat at the back. He considered that a straked wheel was less prone to skidding on wet ground. This would explain why so many tumbrils had broad, straked wheels. Where most other builders were satisfied with $3\frac{1}{2}$ or 4 inch wheels, in South Lincolnshire, they were often fitted with 6 inch hooped wheels, and 6 inch hoops must have required some handling.

Some reference has been made to the large wheels of the early waggons and it has been noted that the overall trend led toward a decrease in size. This trend, however, has been anything but uniform, so that when making any comparisons one is struck by an appreciable variation.

Since wheelwrights were much occupied with the problem of lock, it followed that in many cases, fore wheels decreased more in proportion than the back ones. A few examples will provide an illustration of this. The Oxford had 60 to 62 inch hind wheels and 48 to 57 inch fore wheels, the Somerset Bow had 50 to 58 inch and 42 to 45 inch respectively, the later Dorset had 45 to 55 inch and 37 to 46 inch respectively, while the Large East Anglian had 62 to 69 inch and 43 to 49 inch respectively. Waggons west of the Severn had 53 to 59 inch and 43 to 48 inch respectively. It will be seen that the Oxford was a large-wheeled waggon while the East Anglian had proportionally the smallest front wheels.

Some reference may now be made to variation in track measurement, that is the distance across from near to off, overall. We may not always realise just how bad, and 'permanently' so, was the condition of our roads in times gone by. In some places, such as Salisbury Plain, it was a case of each for himself, in an effort to find a way less deep in ruts. Farm tracks were worse and remained so long after some improvement had been made in the highways. A waggon made its own ruts and in the narrow confines of a lane, made them deeper and deeper till they were literally axle-deep. Such ruts baked hard in summer and set the gauge for any vehicles. In these conditions, it became necessary for waggons to be built to suit the ruts; 'taking the routs' Sturt called it, virtually repeating the comments made 150 years previously . . . that if a waggon did not fit the ruts, it could be 'overset' by one side dropping into the ruts while the other rode high.

Because wheelwrights had always built to their respective precedent, there had been a great variation in the track measurements, from county to county, with the consequence that any waggon could not necessarily be used far from its customary routes. In this matter, the early broad-wheeled types were better off, because they could often roll out the lesser ruts. An indication of the variation in track made can be gained from the following. Oxford 62 to 66 inches, Somerset 65 to 71 inches, Surrey 77 inches, Kent 68 inches, and Yorkshire 50 to 67 inches.

Before leaving the subject of wheels we may note two details. Until quite late in the history of waggon-making it had been the practice to set the spokes in a straight line round the nave. Most spokes were 3½ inches deep, from front to back, at the nave and 3 inches deep at the rim. Toward the end of the nineteenth century it became increasingly common, but by no means universal, to set the spokes in a staggered line around the nave. Many wrights considered this provided a stronger wheel, though others maintained that well-tapered spokes were sufficient.

Even the number of spokes in wheels appear to have been determined by precedent. They always had spoked them 10 and 12 (front and rear) so they went on doing so, regardless of the practice in the next county of spoking 12 and 14. So writers have grouped waggons according to some conspicuous features, such as the degree of lock or the profile of the body. None has done so according to spoking of wheels, although there are considerable areas in which one will find that the wheels were always 10 and 12 or 12 and 14. No Oxford ever had other than 10 and 12. No Kent other than 12 and 14.

THE BODY

The framework of the body consisted originally of two side-members, from front to back, which were joined at each end and midway, by three transverse members. Between the sides, additional lighter members were fitted, equidistantly. On this framework, the sides and head were constructed and the floor-boards laid. The older waggons had the two sides each in one continuous piece, but the later ones had their sides divided, to permit an insection to be made for the front wheels. This will be referred to again under WHEEL-LOCK. In the majority of waggons, the front and middle transverses were lap-jointed to the sides, with the hind transverse morticed to them. In certain county designs, all three trans-verses were morticed. This was always the case in Sussex and Kent.

The early waggons had floor-boards of elm, laid lengthwise to provide a clean surface for a shovel when coal or ballast had to be off-loaded. During the last quarter of the nineteenth century, timber merchants began importing softwood, under the comprehensive term 'deal'. Wheelwrights could henceforth depend upon a supply of planks of uniform thickness. Even so, there was still the possibility of the awkward plank rising above its neighbours, enough to bring the shovel up with a jolt.

The body of a waggon consisted of the arrangement of a number of uprights with one or more horizontal rails, according to the depth of the body, on each side and front. A partial closure of the spaces was effected by placing a number of round spindles or flat bars along the sides and front. In some designs this arrangement was left open but in others it soon became the practice to close the head and sides with panel-boards.

Although the open-sided body apparently was quite satisfactory for farm waggons transporting corn and hay, the road-hauliers must clearly have required panelled bodies—there were long-distance stage-waggons as well as coaches, for the conveyance of passengers with the goods. That open-sided waggons were, however, made for many years, is de-monstrated by the model of a Surrey waggon, c1800, in the Science Museum, London, and made by H. R. Waiting. The author remembers such a waggon, performing its last service to its country as a road-block, at Amberley, Sussex, in 1940.

A kind of hybrid between the 'open' and the 'closed' was produced until comparatively recently by the East Anglian wheelwrights, con-currently with the more usual fully-panelled types. The waggons so made were of medium size, and had panels along the lower half of the head and sides, leaving the top half open. It is of interest that at one time, when panel-boards first came in, they were secured to the spindles by means of greased leathern thongs, a method which was considered superior to the later use of nails, which often worked loose however well they had been clenched.

In most designs of body, the head and sides were a fixture, with the tail-board hinged, either to be dropped down or removed. In certain designs, such as those of East Anglia, the head-board was made re-movable and was pegged in position in the same manner as a tail-board. In other designs, such as the Kent, there was no tail-board at all, but instead a stout bar was pegged in the closed position, across the ends of the top-rails, leaving the end otherwise open. Projecting over the wheels from the top rail of each side a rail ran the full length, to keep the hay or corn clear of the wheels. In many designs this was left open, although there were a number of rods the whole length between the two rails. But in others, this was fitted with a thin plank, sometimes known as a lime-board. In the final designs of waggon, the Boats and the Barges, all this projection was a single piece of plank usually thicker than formerly. These late waggons mostly had their sides similar of one piece planking and were, in fact, collectively termed 'plank-bodied' to distinguish them from the spindle or panelled earlier types.

The arrangement of the component parts of the body varied so much from one county to another, that it was possible to make a positive identification, sometimes almost to the individual wheelwright. These details are dealt with at considerable length in the descriptions of county designs, and the colour plates will provide visual explanation to much of this.

Nearly every waggon had a 'sheer', or a profile rising fore and aft of midway. Some were, in fact, so ship-like that one may be permitted the use of a few nautical terms. Others were box-like and had markedly vertical 'static' lines that did not suggest movement.

To attempt to account for the great variation in appearance between the waggons of West Shropshire and Kent, between Lincolnshire and Dorset, or even among those of Essex alone, would engulf one in fruitless contentions leading nowhere. Better to accept them and to study and enjoy them, as one enjoys villages, churches, or cottages.

All wheelwrights used oak, ash, elm, deal or beech according to local practice, and sometimes immediate availability, for the various wooden parts, and wrought iron for certain kinds of supports and of course for bolts, pins, chains, brackets and tyres. We have noted that the axle-arms when separate from the bed were of case-hardened steel, and also that beech was always preferred for the older axle-trees. The axle-bed was normally of oak, though beech or ash were occasionally used, but ash was nearly always used for the wheel-felloes, for all the rails and the wooden uprights and body supports. Again, without exception, the undercarriage pole, the shafts and fore-carriage hounds were all made of ash. Elm and oak were used for the body frame and elm again for the floor-planks. Some wrights made the body frames wholly of oak and nothing else and selected pitch pine for the panel-boards of sides, head and tail, while others preferred elm. With all these variations, from one wright to another, they all and without exception chose elm for the naves of their wheels and oak for the spokes. Some wrights followed their county tradition of wood, rather than wrought iron for the main standards which supported the body, while others made a change toward iron. Then we shall find that in some counties, such as Oxford, iron was always used.

In each county or region, there were clearly differing ideas concerning dimensions, not only of wheels, as we have seen, but even more of the length, breadth and height of the body. Once a county 'trend' had been established, it became customary and eventually traditional, together with the other features. So it came about that in some counties the bodies were deep, and required two middle rails instead of one, while in others, the bodies were so shallow that not only was the middle rail dispensed with but the hind part of the body had to be arched or bowed, to clear the wheels. This bow, together with a pronounced rise forwards, produced a graceful and ship-like profile, which was in marked contrast with the box-like appearance of the deeper waggons.

In all this vast array of the wheelwright's craft, one may hesitate to declare openly one's preference or to give prominence to any one, to the implied deprecation of any others which were equally lovely in their own way, but it is nevertheless clear that several regions produced waggons which, by their lines and proportions, did attain something like a Golden Mean.

Design and shape and size became very much determined by traditions, which, at their best, eventually produced some very good waggons. However, in the environment of slow change, there was a tendency to distrust new ideas, and to retain the established ones. Some regions arrived at a satisfactory design comparatively early—the Oxford 'got there' during the last years of the eighteenth century and thenceforward changed little and in truth, really did not need to. With a tare weight of about 18 cwt., against the 25 cwt. or more of many others, it had a light draught, ran well and needed little effort to set it in motion—as Mr. Tustian, who farmed near Banbury, once remarked, 'She rol-l-lls'.

We may summarise the appearance of waggons in elevation, by dividing them into two groups. To those with an unbroken, continuous line from front to back, the deeper bodied waggons, we may apply the term 'Sheer-rave'. The second group comprised those which were shallow enough to require some form of arching in order to clear the hind-wheels. Some, such as the Oxfords, had a 'half-bow'; others, like the Wiltshire, had a 'full-bow'. In Somerset and Dorset, where the tail end did not descend behind the wheel there was the 'Cock-rave'.

This distinction was far less important than that affecting the lock, which we shall later consider at length. And because the greater part of a load of hay or corn lay well above the top, the capacity of a waggon did not really depend upon the depth of the body; only when the load was in sacks or consisted of coal or ballast was this the case.

The nature of the land, light or heavy, wet or dry, determined the wheel-treads. At any period in the history of farm-waggons, the variations in tread meant that the age of a waggon could not be easily determined. It very soon became something like a tradition for Oxford waggons to have $2\frac{1}{2}$ inch hoop tyres, whether for use on the Cotswolds or in the Vale of Aylesbury, and for the majority of waggons between Bristol and Shrewsbury to have broad wheels, while in South east England $3\frac{1}{2}$ or 4 inch treads were found on the majority of waggons.

We can investigate practices in all the regions and find sufficient variation to make any conclusions regarding age extremely difficult, although we can say that if an Oxford waggon had square-sectioned, ironwork, then it was pre-1850. This does not follow with other regions, some of which retained square iron to the end or at least continued to use it concurrently with round.

Some regions, such as Oxford, did not simplify their later waggons, while others, such as Somerset, underwent some radical changes from an early elaboration to a quite simple design in which not only the frills disappeared but the colour was changed.

A comparison may be made between the Oxford waggon and the Large Suffolk, shown respectively on Plates 8 and 18. The lightness of the Oxford is quite evident and it is clear that the wheelwrights went as far as they dared, not only by skilful chamfering but by using fewer parts than in the Suffolk. The tare weight of the Oxford, already noted, was 18 cwt. and that of the Suffolk, between 25 and 30 cwt. The Kent, shown on Plate 1, was a heavier waggon than it looked, at 25 cwt.

The capacity of these waggons must now be balanced against their weights. The Oxford ran on $2\frac{1}{2}$ inch wheels and was intended to carry 3 tons of corn in sheaf and be drawn by one horse, or not more than two. The Kent ran on 4 inch wheels, and was intended to carry 5 tons of hops in pocket and be drawn by 4 horses. A single horse is easily managed and will pull well, but four horses, harnessed to one waggon, will not do four times the work of one. In western Shropshire, it was often necessary to use six or even eight horses.

We may be surprised to learn what loads were carried. Some 5 ton waggons were often loaded to 6 when used on the hard road, and the old road-carriers could take as much as 8 tons. Between the extremes of the 'hard road' of the nineteenth century and the soft wet clays, there were varying conditions to be contended with. As far back as 1757, Edward Lisle, of Crux Easton, Hants, wrote in his *Observations in Husbandry*, . . . 'the level surface resistance per 100 lb. gross weight of vehicle (waggon) was 19 on soft land, 9 on corn stubble and 4 on macadam, so that a good road offered a fraction over one-fifth that of plough land.'

The sides of a waggon body were braced at the front by the headboard rail and bracing irons, but the rear end, where the tail-board was a separate, hinged part, was without any bracing. The rear end therefore required other support, and some support was also needed at midway. At these two points, the transverse members projected outward by a foot or so, and were of quite stout proportions, more so in some regions than in others. To these four projections, standards of either wood or iron were inserted to give the necessary support, as flying buttresses in a cathedral. Whatever the material, they were very strong.

Immediately above the front and hind wheels, further support was given by fitting uprights, again of wood or iron, which were secured, bolted or bracketed to the side members. Whether wrought iron was stronger or lasted longer than well-seasoned ash can be disputed, but in practice, it was county precedent which had the say. In Oxfordshire they used iron, in Northamptonshire wood, and in another part of the country, they used both on one waggon. It was a point of identification. The result of this multiple bracing and support was a rigid body, fully able to carry its load without the eventual 'bellying' we too often see on the modern open motor-lorry.

As with other waggon parts, the shape of these supports became very much a tradition with each county, so much so that one could glance at a waggon and tell by its standards alone, to which county it belonged.

There was no mistaking the iron 'Y' of Wiltshire, the wooden 'wish-bone' of Shropshire, the 'elbow' of Herefordshire, the 'N' of Kent, or the 'cupids' bow of Sussex.

These standards and the top-rail of the head-board, between them gave support to the projecting rails or boards. The extremities of the iron standards were threaded to take square nuts and the feet of the standards passed right through the beams and were secured with large nuts and the tops similarly passed through the rails and in turn were secured. Wooden standards had their feet inserted in mortices cut in the beams and in this position were secured by carriage bolts. Wooden intermediate supports of wood were secured by either iron brackets or bolts, to the floor sides. Iron supports were always bolted.

It has been noted that at one time a great deal of square-sectioned iron was used and it was then customary for the blacksmith to give some vent to his artistry by giving these bars a spiral twist while still hot. The length of this spiral naturally depended on the distance between any two points of support. When the later round-section iron came into use, these delightful forms of decoration could not be incorporated.

Before Whitworth established standard threads, the village smiths used to tap their own, and it often happened that nuts and bolts made by different smiths could not be interchanged. Some of the very early waggons had their ironwork secured by metal keys which were tapped into slots and it seems likely that many wheelwrights were not too happy with this method and therefore preferred the ash standards. Every component part of a waggon was so well made and fitted together that in the event of subsequent wear or breakage, the damaged part could be extracted and a new one put in its place. The best made waggons were reasonably free from failure of any part, but accidents did happen.

WHEEL LOCK

One often comes across reference to 'the old quarter-locks', a term which requires some explanation. The writers, in referring to 'quarter', 'half', 'three-quarters', and 'full-lock', mean the amount by which the front wheels could swivel before being stopped by contact with the body. It meant that a quarter-lock waggon required a greater circle in which to turn round than a half-lock and that a full-lock required the smallest circle of all. Although these terms were satisfactory in the broad sense,

they inadequately described the range of turning-circles, from over 50 feet down to little more than the length of the body. The terms were related more to the shape of the body frame, whether or not it had an insection, than to the diameter of the circle.

All the early waggons had straight sides, from front to back—'straight-bed' they were called—and with their large wheels they did require a wide circle in which to turn and in consequence of this they could prove awkward in a limited space. Such writers of that time as Marshall were extremely critical and many wheelwrights sought to overcome this problem which was greater for farm-waggons than for road-carriers.

It will be realised that in turning in the shortest possible circle the inside fore-wheel of a straight-bed waggon, or quarter-lock, will make contact with the side of the body. To prevent the consequent chafing and wearing away of the timber, wheelwrights had two remedies. The most satisfactory was the fitment of chains each side, between the axle-bed and next the nave and to some part of the body-frame. By this means the swivel of the axle-bed was restricted by the one chain being pulled taut while its opposite number fell slack. As a further precaution iron plates were fitted to the frame where the chafing would occur. Such plates, or cleats, were replaceable.

Wrights were still averse to decreasing the diameter of the fore-wheels on the grounds that this would increase the draught. But they did appreciate that if the body were made narrower at the offending part, it would be possible to obtain a shorter lock. Some wheelwrights divided the side-members into two parts, fore and aft of the middle beam, turning the fore-side in to join the beam as much as six or seven inches behind the hind-side which was left straight. This entailed searching for timber with the right curve. All the waggons of South-east England and East Anglia thus became insected or waist-bed. In Oxfordshire, they effected a compromise by overlapping the fore- and hind-sides which gave an insection equal to the thickness of the hind member. It was called a crooked-bed.

The proportions of the Oxford were so well devised that this design came to be recognised as one of the best on all considerations, and it continued to be produced in large numbers with no more than detail variant, for the next 150 years. Marshall certainly expressed his approval and recommended its universal adoption, but of course, that was asking a little too much where precedent played such a decisive part.

In the face of this attitude, the Boat and Barge waggons were introduced late in the nineteenth century to sweep aside all the long-standing precepts and, too, any objection to change. Although the first of the new designs were partly restricted in turning by the retention of the tongue-pole, the fore-wheels of most were small enough so that when the pole was dispensed with the final designs of both Boat and Barge waggons were fully-locking.

If the fore-wheels of the older waggons were large enough so that in locking they only brushed the sides, then the locking-cleat was probably sufficient and may have explained the absence of chains on some waggons. But if the wheels came only a little above the underside of the floor then they could and did easily wedge themselves tight under the floor. The provision of chains obviated this.

There were at least three systems of restriction by chains. The most commonly adopted consisted of a chain each side of the fore-bolster which ran back to a suitable point in front of the middle beam or on the beam itself. The second, which was peculiar to some of the Hereford waggons, consisted also of a chain each side, and attached as in the first system, to the fore-bolster but running right back to the hind axle-bed. Both chains were suspended at three intermediate points to prevent their swaying and fouling when slack. The third system, used on some of the waggons of Wessex, consisted of a short chain hanging from each side and above the rear part of the fore-carriage hounds to which the chains were secured. They gave a jingling accompaniment to the click-clack-click of the wheels.

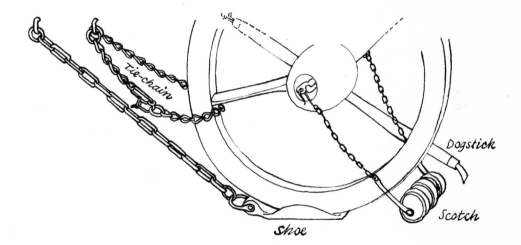

TYPES OF BRAKE

There were three kinds. One for descending a hill; a second for ascent; and a third which was used when the waggon was stationary. The first retarded the descent by means of a shoe, which was bolted on the end of a chain from the middle beam or thereabouts and which at full stretch, allowed the shoe to lie between the rim of the wheel and the ground. The shoe thus carried the wheel and slid along the ground. The second type prevented the waggon from running back should the horses stop. There were two kinds, one consisting of a small roller on a spindle attached to two chains, one of which hung from the waggon and the second being hooked to an eye in the nearside axle linch-pin so the roller

19

followed very close behind the wheel. When not in use, it was hooked out of the way under the floor. This roller-brake was the more common of the two, but there was an alternative in the form of an ash stick with a pronged tip. This dog-stick was permanently hinged at the opposite end to the axle-bed and when out of use, rested in a hook. In use, it was dropped to the ground to trail along. Should the waggon stop, the pronged tip dug in the road-surface and held the waggon. Many Oxford waggons were equipped with this type.

The third brake, for standing, consisted of two lengths of chain which hung from a point just behind the middle beam. When required, the two lengths were passed around the felloe ring and coupled together.

This equipment of brakes varied from region to region. In some, all three types, the shoe, the roller and the tie-chain were fitted. In others, the dog-stick replaced the roller, while in still other regions, the tie-chain alone was fitted and used for all purposes. It was usual to fit these brakes on the nearside, but very often the tie-chain was fitted to both sides on the one waggon; this was so in those regions where broad-wheels continued to be used. A shoe large enough to suit a six inch tread would have been cumbersome, and a roller would not have kept its place well behind a wheel with protruding nails. In those regions where the broad wheel remained in favour, the majority of roads were un-metalled and many were extremely rough. On such roads, broad wheels just crunched and rolled their way, probably better than any narrow wheel. Waggons which were used in flat country, with no ascents and descents to be encountered, were often equipped with tie-chains alone since a standing brake was sufficient.

LADDERS, POLES AND FRAMES, ETC.

There were several ways of increasing the capacity of a waggon when necessary. The most common was a pair of frames or ladders, which could be fitted to the front and back of the body. In most cases, the front ladder fitted onto the fore part of the rails, between the top and the outer. In others, the ladders rested against the head and tail-boards, inside the body, with their feet at floor-level. In many designs, the tail-ladder fitted at floor-level, with the feet at floor-level and resting on the hind-beam. This entailed the removal of the tail-board.

In both Sussex and Kent, and in several other parts, they set tall ash poles at each corner and to secure the load firmly, a long rope was tied to the front and thrown clear over the top to the back, where it was wound tight on a windlass, which was a fixture under the hind-beam. They sometimes used poles in Herefordshire, but nearly every waggon there was supplied complete with a harvest-frame always referred to in the plural—thripples. This frame was in two parts, which overhung the body all round and met midway, where they were secured together: the use of thripples explains the absence of projecting rails from some waggons.

In the West Midlands generally, they fitted fenders or cratches to sides and front, to deepen the body by some nine inches. These fenders were often beautifully made, and fitted accurately. Such fenders were also used in Lincolnshire. In Wales, all gambos were fitted with poles, as often as not, taken straight from the coppice.

North and South Lincolnshire, surprisingly, were not only distinctive by their respective designs of waggon, but by their loading equipment. The fenders of North Lincs, that is, Kesteven and Lindsey, have been noted, but in the south, that is Holland, where the principle load was potatoes, a high semi-open framework, like a tall fender, was preferred. This went in all round the body, and was also used when transporting sheep and pigs, in order to deter any attempt at jumping overboard during the journey.

CHAMFERING

If every wooden member of a waggon had been left in its original square section, the result would have been an unnecessarily heavy vehicle. It was George Sturt, the Surrey wheelwright, who estimated that about one-eighth of the original weight of timber in his waggons was eliminated by chamfering and that this could be accomplished without loss of strength. This process using a drawknife along all exposed edges, left a bevelled edge between the joints.

Wheelwrights naturally sought to transform this elementary bevelling into something which was more satisfying to the eye. The waggon, apart from its functions, was already a thing of beauty, which could be enhanced by a little exercise with a drawknife. It may be thought that some went further than need be, but pride in the job decreed it worth the time and effort and the results were remarkable for the artistry in their creation. In some regions, it reached a very fine level, while in others, there seemed little attempt beyond the elementary.

In some waggons, the square edge was transformed into a quarter circle, with a concave step-up at each end, where the square was retained for a joint. This chamfering was often so extensive that there was hardly a square section of wood left. It was on the axle-beds and bolsters, and the fore-carriage hounds that the best work was to be found. One has to see this work and run one's fingers over it to appreciate it fully. Only the shafts were left in the square, supported as they were by bracing at the butt end alone, three-quarters and more of their length extending without support. The strength of the blades depended upon the spring of ash and its resistance to shock.

Along a broad, irregular belt across England, from the Golden Cap in Dorset to the Wash on the East Coast, there was scarcely a waggon made which was not noticeable for the chamfering. In many parts, pride in the making was followed by pride of ownership and it was often a matter of prestige that a farmer's waggons be maintained in a first-class condition. He could not afford to have his name exhibited on a broken waggon, badly in need of repair. It was good business all round.

Between there and the Thames, the waggons of East Anglia were comparatively simply treated. To the west of the Severn, the work blossomed forth in its own right, particularly in the Clun area of West Shropshire, just where one might perhaps have expected simplicity. The Hereford waggons too, though less ornate on the body work, could show some remarkable work on the undercarriages.

The older waggons of Somerset and Dorset were readily to be identified by their chamfer-work and hardly less beautiful were those of Oxfordshire, though the general appearance and ornament was simpler. In Northamptonshire, the work matched the standard of head-board painting and although to some eyes much of it seems a little excessive, yet I never heard of a waggon built at Flore suffering breakage owing to weakness in structure.

COLOURS OF WAGGONS AND BRANDING

There were traditional colours of the body for each county or region —blue for Sussex, yellow for Oxford, orange for Holland, and so on. At the same time, in some regions there was enough variation from tradition that it was sometimes difficult for a student to establish the normal without a lengthy study. One could be sure enough when 111 Oxfords out of 116 were yellow, but in East Anglia, including Essex and Cambridge, where no less than eight colours were recorded, 62% were blue and 22% green. In Herefordshire there certainly were more blues than ochres and yellows, but just to complicate matters, there were four different blues—Prussian, indigo, cobalt and a peacock green-blue. While South Lincolnshire waggons were orange and North Lincolnshire were indigo, those built in the city were either maroon or buff.

One often reads of the undercarriage and wheels as being red, but after making allowance for weathering, of sun, frost and mud, which will in time affect the best paints, that red could be red-oxide, vermilion or salmon orange, according to region. It was noticeable that as one travelled from east to west, across England to Wales, so there was a transition through these reds. In some regions orange, as for the body, was favoured, and in others, maroon.

We may presume that the practice of displaying the owners' names and addresses began when waggons were built with areas of panelling large enough to carry these particulars. As with the shapes of waggons and their decoration, the style of display acquired a county trend and became fairly consistent as the best painters set the standard.

Some designs of waggon left no space on either the head or the tail for this display, but in any case, it was always customary to place identity of ownership on the fore offside. This was usually in white on a black rectangle. It was done, irrespective of any other indication and was as plain as a registration plate. Even this, however, was subject to variation. It was common practice among many painters to write the particulars directly on the panel. In the area between Gloucester and Shrewsbury, the lettering was in black on a long white strip placed just below the top rail. Or the strip may have been black with white lettering.

The styles of lettering and decoration showed early Victorian and Regency influences, which lasted through the century and only in a few cases gave place to the ill-proportioned Edwardian forms. Sometimes this was more due to the accident of a good man being succeeded by a less able one. Until recently, 'Victorian' has been synonymous with arrogance and bad taste, so that one may be agreeably surprised, on perusal of a county directory, set and printed 'locally' in the period 1850 to 1880. The design of type is excellent and the display quite clear and uncluttered. The contrast is remarkable when comparison is made with a similar directory for 1905.

Wheelwrights were slow to change and that being so, it seems likely from the styles that branding was hardly made before the beginning of the nineteenth century. The styles of lettering employed in the paint-shops were derived from examples to be seen everywhere. There was Didot, a boldly stressed letter with fine serifs; Egyptian, a bold block-letter with slab-serifs, which closely resembled the name-plates on Great Western Railway locomotives; a bold sans-serif letter which we now call Grotesque; a fine Italic script and a Black-letter, sometimes known as Old English. Most of this lettering was finished off with right-hand, or left-hand shading.

In most counties this display was fairly restrained and in some cases was extremely plain, but in certain regions the painters really let themselves go. There appeared to be little relationship between cost and effort, and this tendency was admirably continued in a number of counties until the last waggons were built. In Somerset and Dorset, in Northamptonshire and Holland and in the extreme west of Hereford-shire, the painters all attained a brilliant standard. Here and there, one came across an instance where the painter seemed uncertain of himself, but in the main, the work constituted a lively expression. The lining out of chamfered parts was commonly practised in certain regions, particularly in the East Midlands and was consistent with the quality of the chamfering.

When one considers the immense and justifiable pride in the wheel-wrights' craft, it is surprising how few gave any identity on their waggons. A few fixed a plate of cast iron, or enamelled steel to some part of the body, while others wrote their names in the corner of the head or side panels. Those makers who fitted oil lubricated axles had their names incised on the polished metal caps which were screwed on to each arm. In certain counties they made a great display, with the owner's particulars on the head-board and their own on the tail. A few made a display on the head-board containing both owner and maker.

Each wheelwright who did acknowledge his work kept to his estab-lished form of identity and so his waggons were easily recognised. One knew what to look for and where. In all the other cases, it was often either extremely difficult or impossible to establish the origin, and in such cases the only clues were certain characteristics of ornament which were peculiar to any one wheelwright. Even the farmers did not always know, especially when a waggon in question had passed through more than one owner.

Many waggons carried a date on the head-board, but in nearly every case this indicated when the waggon was last painted. I remember a splendid old broad-wheeler, down in the heart of Sussex. The branding read 'J. Boniface. 1888. West Grinstead', but that date indicated when the waggon was last painted. It was, understandably, a little weathered and faded. But there were exceptions. For example, Phillips, of Flore, near Weedon, always *incised* the building date and no amount of re-painting could obliterate it.

Those wheelwrights painted their waggons very well. A good priming was followed by two coats of lead paint which was then varnished. Some added a little gold size. The intervals between painting depended upon the nature of the owner, the best of whom had their waggons repainted at regular intervals, while others just let things go on until something had to be done. After 25 years, all the sun, wind, rain, frost and mud-cake of those years naturally caused·some fading. Blues became violet grey, while the reds turned a whitish-pink, but a rub with a wet rag would usually reveal something of the original colour. No spray-gun could lay the coat that was obtained and demanded then. While they did not seek the finish obtained by the coach-builders and the railway companies, when the last brush-stroke had been applied and the varnish was touch dry, there came the proud day when the waggon was wheeled forth into the open for every passer-by to admire.

After that, the future of the waggon rested with the owner. One man might neglect his waggon from the outset, only being reminded when the ungreased wheels began shrieking in protest. Another might take such care, that 120 years later his great-grandson would treat it as a family heirloom. I know several such waggons. Too often though, a waggon, outdated by the changes in farming, is either left to rot among the nettles, or chopped up 'for the kids' bonfire'.

BOAT AND BARGE WAGGONS

The advent of these waggons has already been mentioned. There were certain differences between the two types, the most important of which was the respective depths of body. The Boat was always shallow in the body, the sides of which were each made of two long boards or planks, the upper being more inclined outward than the lower. Most Barges were fairly deep and resembled a simplified form of the traditional designs. The Boat and Barge differed also in regard to the head- and tail-boards, which in the Boat, were set athwart the sides, where the heads and tails of the Barge were between the sides. The Boat was in fact, a radical departure from all the preceding designs, and it is possible that this accounted for the limited area of distribution in the Waggon Zone. The Barge waggons, much less standardised, penetrated almost everywhere in one form or another. Their makers deliberately copied, in simple forms, the designs of county waggons, where practicable. The Bristol W. and C.W. catalogue of about 1900, showed a Gloucester, a West of England, a Wiltshire and a Midlands waggon, all different, but each available in a capacity range from $1\frac{1}{2}$ to 5 tons, running on wheels of $2\frac{1}{4}$ to 6 inch tread—even here the broad wheel had to be accommodated.

Boat waggons were built by Taskers, of Andover; Rose, of Hungerford; Wilder, of Wallingford; Barrett, of Wroughton, near Swindon, and others at Basingstoke and Deanshanger, near Stony Stratford. It was very much a 'Southern England' waggon. Barge waggons were made by such firms as Crosskill, of Beverley, Yorks; The Bristol Works Ltd.; and David Giles and John Martin, both of Bromsgrove. All these firms were turning out tumbrils in even larger numbers, although none of the products was any better than the best which were then, and until quite recently, being built by the 'small' man. Bysouth, of Braughing, in Hertfordshire won prizes with his tumbrils, and Bingham, of Long Sutton, Lincs, made a Scotch Cart with fixed or drop sides.

The small load, $2\frac{1}{2}$ tons, which the Boat carried may also have weighed literally against the type, especially among farmers accustomed to loading the old waggons up to 6 tons. At the same time, a small waggon could often prove very useful. During the present century, many of the small firms turned to the manufacture of waggons of similar designs, to meet the changing conditions.

Although waggons have often been called by the county of their origin, such as Sussex, Glamorgan, Yorkshire, their distribution has by no means been confined to the boundaries of their respective counties. There was a great deal of overlapping between adjacent counties. This was usually because one design proved more suitable than its neighbour. When one bears in mind that basic designs were determined primarily by the types of terrain and the farming, this dominance and recession appears logical. But then we find, elsewhere, that a particular design has been distributed over two or more counties and on radically differing types of terrain. The West of England Bow waggon was distributed almost without variants throughout Somerset, Dorset and East Devon. The Oxford, eminently suited to the Coltswolds, was extremely numerous in the Vale of Aylesbury. The large, deep-bodied waggon of the East Midlands was in general use everywhere between Banbury, King's Lynn and Boston, that is on both the ironstone Cotswolds—side by side with the Oxfords—and the fenland of the Wash.

It is important to appreciate that although a county design may be recognisable by a number of features, there were the inevitable variations from county practice. The typical Oxford was yellow, had half-bow raves and a crooked bed and ran on narrow wheels, but there were those which were blue or brown, or full-bowed, or had waist-beds, or had broad wheels, but no one Oxford had all these features. Such a waggon would belong to Berkshire. One can go through all the counties and find exceptions. Sometimes one might wonder which was the exception and which the rule. One cannot say that the waggons of this or that county never had such and such a feature, only that it was not typical.

KENT

The waggons of Kent may perhaps be regarded as among the 'plain Janes', and like such Janes, they had their appeal. They were well-designed, thoroughly practical and robust enough to stand up to all the hard work for which they were made.

Throughout the county there was little variation in details, and uniformity was extremely marked. They were made in a variety of sizes, to carry from 30 cwt. on 2 inch wheels to 5 tons on $4\frac{1}{2}$ inch wheels, and the largest were intended to be drawn by four horses, when fully laden with hops or corn. Although the makers were prepared to supply double-shafts, they were usually fitted with single-shafts, which were always secured by a pin to the fore-carriage.

The medium depth body was deeply waisted with all three transverse floor members morticed to the sides. From the middle standard, the top and out-rails rose fore and aft in a straightish line—this, in most waggons is a gentle sheer. The straight lines were accentuated by the vertical trend of all uprights and by the N shaped iron standards. The only relief was in the curves of the front edges of the side panel-boards. Without exception every waggon body had only one summer between the frames. Middle side-rails were never present except in 'hybrids', but the panelling on the sides was repeated on the front. This was made up of 10 to 12 flat spars on the sides and 3 or 4 on the front. No Kent was ever made with a tail-board, but in its place was a wooden bar, pegged across the rail-ends. Below the hind-beam, or dware, a rope roller was usually fitted, by which a rope, thrown over the load from the front, could be drawn tight. Every waggon was built with the outrails closed by boards. The full load was contained by vertical poles, set in brackets at the corners. For the convenience of the carter, a waggon box was fitted, usually on the front board but sometimes on the near side, just in front of the middle standard.

Every waggon had 12 spokes in the front wheels and 14 in the back. While the majority had 4 inch wheels, there were nearly as many with $3\frac{1}{2}$ inch treads. The writer has no record, among nearly 90 waggons noted, of any with broad wheels or even narrow ones with strakes. Most of them had greased axles, but Pope, of Chiddingstone, built waggons which were lubricated with oil. The metal axle-caps were incised with his name. A few very old waggons were noted with wooden arms. An instance of 'hybridisation' may be noted in that W. J. Tedham, of Bodiam, in Sussex, built his waggon according to the Kent design, without mid-raves.

Except along the boundary between Kent and Sussex, waggons were usually painted a colour which varied from cream to pale ochre, but in fact, some 25% of all recorded were finished in the same blue as Sussex waggons. Every one had the undercarriage finished in a red-oxide or deep vermilion. Both the body and the undercarriage were devoid of any lining-out. Branding on the head-board was hardly known but exceptionally was done by Heathfield, of Ashford, one of whose waggons, built for J. Henley, of Pattenden Farm, Goudhurst, represents the county on Plate 1. Kent Waggons never carried the owner's name on a black plate, as in most counties, but the particulars were set out in small sans-serif letters in a continuous line over the middle standard, either on the out-rail or the top-rail.

KENT

Built by Heathfield of Ashford.

Owned by J. Henley, of Pattenden Farm, Goudhurst.

Plate 1

SUSSEX

The waggons of this county had the same deep waist as those of Kent and also the front, middle and hind beams were all joined to the sides by mortice and tenon joints. The sides of the body had a middle rail and 16 to 18 spindles or a lesser number of spars. In the majority of waggons this arrangement was repeated on the head-board, but a few had plain boards. The iron standards had a gentle cyma curve to the down stroke of the N, unlike the straight one of the Kent. Some 35% of waggons had a pair of wooden supports above each wheel indicating a transition toward, or from, Surrey. The remaining 65% had similar pairs but of iron, shaped like 'cupids' bows, similar to many Surrey waggons.

There was a greater variety to be noted with regard to the wheels. Where all Kents had 12 spokes in front and 14 in the rear, only 33% of Sussexes had this spoking, the majority having the wheels spoked 10 and 12. The treads varied from $2\frac{1}{2}$ to 6 inch but the majority had 4 inch. There appeared to be little connection between the tread-width and the terrain, as all widths were encountered on both Down and Weald. The wheel diameters appeared to be fairly uniform, about 48 inch for the front and 58 for the back and therefore similar to the Kent. The brakes consisted of shoe, tie-chain and scotch. Corner-poles were fitted at harvest-time and the load was secured by a rope, passed over the top from front to back and wound tight on a rope-roller, fitted under the hind-beam. Lock-chains were nearly always provided.

Many Sussex waggons had no tail-board, the back being partly closed by a wooden bar, pegged in position across the ends of the top-rails. These latter, unlike the Kent, were left open and were doubled. Chamfering was quite simple though more developed than on the Kent waggons. Without exception the Sussex waggons were painted Prussian blue with red-oxide or vermilion undercarriages.

The waggon illustrated on Plate 2 was an interesting example of the older broad-wheel kind. It was built for John Boniface of West Grinstead.

In one respect, this waggon was almost unique in that the tongue-pole had no side braces to the hind-carriage. The wheels ran on wooden arms. The red head-panel was not common in the county and the West Sussex trend of the waggon was emphasised by the normal hinged tail-board. This waggon bore no maker's identity, but a few makers, such as Woolgar of East Grinstead and Horder of Loxwood did fit plates.

Sussex waggons were numerous and generally distributed over the whole of East Sussex, but in diminishing numbers in West Sussex as one travelled toward Hampshire, and where the Sussex was in company with both the Surrey—made by Horder—and the Hampshire waggons. Reference to intermingling with Kent, Surrey and Hampshire waggons does not imply that the Sussex was a hybrid. Rather was Sussex a centre from which some sound ideas radiated. Deep in the heart of the county and among the Downland farms there was no mistaking that waggon. It somehow looked bigger than its neighbours even though it may not have been. It had a graceful sheer, and the double outraves and the middle rave may have helped the deception.

Among a host of wheelwrights, there was Weller, of Sompting; Edwards and Brett, both of Forest Row; and the cousins Tedham, W. J. of Bodiam and Frank of Northiam, as well as those already mentioned.

Some 28 years ago, I encountered a giant of a waggon at Amberley. It had a straight bed and the body was without panelling but consisted of top and middle raves all round and a large number of upright spindles. The sides were braced by a similar structure forming the head and supported by iron standards at the middle and hind beams. It was designed to carry double shafts. It was similar in general arrangement to the model of a Surrey waggon dated from about 1800 and has been referred to under the heading BODIES.

SUSSEX

Owned by John Boniface, of West Grinstead.

Plate 2

SURREY

The semi-absorption of Surrey into the conurbation of Greater London will not help us to realise that at one time the county was as rural as any other. There are, however, in many parts of the county away from London, still considerable areas of farming, especially in those parts adjacent to Sussex. It was also the native county of George Sturt.

It is a matter of conjecture as to the appearance of the waggons of those days. In the description of the Sussex waggons, reference is made to the Surrey waggon of about 1800 and it seems likely to have been representative of the waggons of that time but it gives no hint of ancestry to the later kind now called a Surrey, and still less to the Sussex. The late Surreys had no apparent 'roots' in the Weald, but were more closely related to those of Hampshire and, to some extent even Dorset. It was, in fact a West Surrey waggon. East Surrey is bounded so closely by Kent and Sussex that it is likely that the waggons there were quite strongly influenced by their neighbours.

Although the Surrey waggons had very little affinity with those of Sussex, they were quite common in the west of that county, where the Sussex waggon was, surprisingly enough, less common than in East Sussex. Surrey waggons also penetrated into north-east Hampshire and it is not without interest that at least one Sussex wheelwright, Horder of Loxwood, built many waggons to the Surrey design.

All the waggons had straight-beds and when looked at from the side, they showed a slight 'fore and aft rake' which was more suggestive of the west than the south-east. The sides had middle raves and about 17 spindles and were supported by iron standards and a pair of wood staves—Sturt called them strouters—over each wheel. An iron stay curved up from each to support the open out-raves, which were double. While the staves were flatly cupid's-bowed, like the Sussex, the iron standards were distinctive, whereby two square rods spread up from a common foot, one to rise almost vertically to the outer raves, while the

other turned over to meet the top rail of the side. The whole side had a very gentle sheer to front and back.

A further point of distinction from the south-eastern waggons was the normal lap-jointing of the front and middle beams. The head-panel was set flush with the sides and the top rail, and was almost invariably painted red with the branding in bold letters.

Some waggons had paired shafts, which were joined by a splinter-bar to the fore-carriage, while others had single shafts, secured by the simple draught-pin. Very few had broad wheels, but the narrow ones, either $2\frac{1}{2}$ inch or 3 inch, were similar in diameter to the Sussex and Hampshire, about 46 inch and 58 inch, front and back. They were only slightly dished and had 10 spokes in the front and 12 in the back. Straked-wheels disappeared very early, though Sturt stated that as late as 1884, they had not been quite superseded by hoop-tyres. The waggons were fitted with all three brakes, the shoe, the scotch and the tie-chain, but dog-sticks were sometimes fitted in the place of scotches. Ladders were supplied to be fitted at the front to the top rails and to the floor-side at the back. All Surreys were fitted with a tail-board but none recorded had a rope-roller.

It has been stated elsewhere that the bodies were painted brown or buff, but in fact, Sturt's waggons were all Prussian blue and this colour was certainly more common. Nevertheless, some waggons were buff or ochre, and there was one of this colour on a farm between Thursley and Hindhead. The undercarriages were always red. Colour apart, there appears to have been a considerable uniformity in the general arrangement. The making has been described in *The Wheelwright's Shop*. The waggon shown on Plate 3 is a good example of the work of Sturt and Goacher, of Farnham. Sturt considered it to have been built, in its original state, before 1865, but the lettering is of a much later date, about 1920. It was noted on a farm at Elvetham, near Fleet, Hampshire.

SURREY

Built by Sturt and Goacher, of Farnham.

Owned by Henry Lunn, Elvetham, near Odiham, Hants.

Plate 3

HAMPSHIRE

There appear to have been at least two distinct designs of waggon made in Hampshire. In the eastern half of the county, between Fareham and Basingstoke there were two variants of one design distinctive enough to be regarded as 'native'. One was made at Alton, by Hetherington and the second by Etheridge, at Bishop's Waltham.

Both waggons were straight-bed, with an appreciable sheer, more forward than to rear. The designs appeared to incorporate, successfully, a number of features from other counties without loss of identity. From Dorset came the four summers and the shallow body. From nearby Farnham, in Surrey, came the arrangement of 20 spindles, and even distant Sussex may have suggested the iron cupid's bows, in pairs over each wheel. The plain head-boards were set between the projecting ends of the side panel-boards, each of which had ornamental edges. The tail-boards, however were panelled and hinged with 'barrel-eyes'. The out-rails were double, as in Surrey and Dorset and were well-supported by iron stays. The iron standards were V shaped with the outer rod slightly curved. The front and middle beams were lap-jointed.

Most waggons had their shafts hinged by splinter-bar to the four hounds of the carriage but there were many on which the simple draught-pin was used with a two-hound carriage. Most of the Alton waggons had turn-table rings fitted to the fore-carriage bolster and pillow. The wheels were all narrow, usually $2\frac{1}{2}$ inches, slightly dished, and there were 12 spokes in the front and 14 in the back. This is a little surprising, as both Dorsets and Surreys were spoked 10 and 12 but the braking was similar to all south coast waggons, with shoe, tie-chain and either scotch or dog-stick. Some of the Alton waggons had a rope-roller fitted to the hind ladder, which fitted at floor-level, while the fore ladder was at the usual position, on top of the body.

The Alton waggons were to be distinguished by the crooked pin which closed the front end of each side, and which 'missed' the front beam to pass through the side member, behind it. Most of them carried a maker's plate of cast iron, a parallelogram shaped to fit snugly at the bottom of the side close to the fore-end. Some had a very shallow box, similar to the Kent, on the near side, and some also had pole-braces of iron instead of wood. It is possible that the ochre bodies which were noted on the Hampshire-Surrey-Sussex border were influenced by the ochre of Hetherington's waggons. These had heads and tails painted red with the branding on the head-panel. All chamfered edges were usually picked out in blue with the red wheels lined in black. The lettering was quite plain, either in white shaded blue or black.

The really distinctive feature of the waggons built at Bishop's Waltham was the head-board, which was set widely athwart the sides. The top rail was at least three inches deep and very nicely chamfered and like all southern waggons had a concave curve. Both sides of the head-board had elaborately carved edges and the centre part of the board, which carried the branding was sunk by an inch or so. In the remaining parts the Waltham and Alton waggons were similar. The waggon shown on Plate 4 was one of two, built by Hetherington, for William Brock and Son, of West Worldham, which lies between Alton and Selborne.

In the Curtiss Museum, at Alton, there is a very fine model of the second design of waggon such as was used in the north west of the county, where Berkshire and Wiltshire meet. This waggon is readily to be distinguished from the first design on every feature. There is little of Wiltshire but a lot of Berkshire in the general arrangement. It has a waist-bed and the sides are without any mid-raves and the arrangement of the spindle is wholly 'Berkshire'. Likewise the fully-bowed out-raves which are treble, possibly the only instance of this. The ladders are fairly large and in the Wiltshire manner are set between the body-sides to anchor in floor eyes. They rise nearly vertically but curve up to the vertical, where the Wiltshire are straight. The final 'break' with Hampshire is the yellow body.

WILLIAM BROCK & SON

WEST WORLDHAM HANTS

HAMPSHIRE

Built by Hetherington, of Alton.

Owned by William Brock and Son, West Worldham, near Selborne.

Plate 4

THE EARLIER WAGGONS OF THE WEST OF ENGLAND

Plate 5 shows one of the 'cock-raved' waggons which were built by many wheelwrights. This example was made by Cummins, of Bridgwater, for A. Edwards, of Boundary Farm, Glastonbury and was found with three of the later 'sheer-raved' type.

The older waggons appeared, perhaps by deception, to be a little larger than the later ones, which were appreciably shorter in the body and lower than most waggons. They had quite large wheels, some of which had 5 inch treads. The 'cock-raved' design was easily to be distinguished from the half- or full-bowed by the manner in which the raves rose over the hind wheels, not to descend behind them but to turn up again in a flourish. The whole effect was suggestive of the stern of an early sailing ship. The raves were usually double and left open.

The sides were panelled, with middle raves and about 16 spars or spindles. Wood was used for all the supports, at middle- and hind-beam and over the wheels. There was a decided fore and aft rake to the positioning of the staves and supports, indicating an affinity with some of the waggons of South Gloucestershire.

The head- and tail-boards were identical in shape and were set well athwart the sides which were in turn set wider than most waggons. This breadth, together with the sides which were no more than 12 inches deep, midway, made the bodies appear very shallow indeed. The tail-boards were hinged 'pin and eye' for quick removal. Almost without exception four summers were the rule, a feature retained to the very end when quite simple waggons were being built.

These older waggons were remarkable for the standard of chamfer-work and the decoration generally. Every wooden support, the fore-carriage, the beams and the head- and tail-board were exquisitely treated and by this alone one could identify them. All the ironwork was made from square bar, never round, and was given a spiral twist.

Most of these waggons had single shafts, attached by draught-pin to four hounds. Except for a few 5 inch wheels, all were narrow, only slightly dished and set to a fairly wide track, usually about 70 inches. The carriage-pole was extended back to join the hind-beam. The wheels all had 10 spokes in the front and 12 in the back.

Very large, Wiltshire-type ladders were set between the sides of the straight-bed body. Braking was by shoe, tie-chain and scotch, but in a few instances by tie-chain alone.

The bodies were painted Prussian blue with yellow centre-panels on head and tail on which the branding was placed, the owner on the front and the maker on the tail, together with the date. Some waggons had green panels with yellow lettering, but those with yellow panels had the lettering in black, shaded blue or red, or in red, shaded black. After about 1870, the trend towards simplicity in structure and decoration began.

Among a host of remarkable wheelwrights, the following should be mentioned—Vincent, of Ham; Rossiter, of Crewkerne, who served his apprenticeship under Vincent; Cox of Dundon; Richards of Stoborough; Kail, of Horton; Kiddle, of East Stour; Hardy, of Durweston; Gill, of Exmouth; Forsey, of Symondsbury, Bridport; and Milford, of Thorverton. There is a fine example of one of these waggons, made near Cullompton, at the Museum of English Rural Life.

SOMERSET

Built by Cummins, of Bridgwater.

Owned by A. Edwards, of Glastonbury.

Plate 5

THE LATER WAGGONS OF SOMERSET, DORSET AND DEVON

During the last years of the nineteenth century, the wheelwrights in this region were building the new sheer-raved waggons concurrently with the old cock-raved bow-waggon. In consequence of this practice, it was often possible to find examples of both designs by the same maker on one farm. Such was the case at Moorbath Farm, Symondsbury, near Bridport. Here, they were both made by Forsey, of Symondsbury, for Joseph Gibbs. And likewise at Boundary Farm, Glastonbury, where A. Edwards owned waggons built by Cummins, of Bridgwater.

At first, the new waggons were hardly less ornate than the old. All the detail characteristics were retained, the body shallow still, but with a sheer much less pronounced, and the middle raves and wood supports at the middle and rear beams and over both wheels all beautifully chamfered in the traditional manner. The head- and tail-boards were similar and were set athwart the sides. The out-raves, left open as before, were now usually single instead of double and were supported by round-section stays as often as the square. Much would depend upon a wheelwright's stock of bars. Tail-boards, as before, were hinged 'pin-and-eye' and the practice of putting four summers in the frame was continued.

Many of these waggons had splinter-bars on fore-carriage and shafts, which was a departure. Where the draught-pin anchorage was retained, some carriages had two hounds instead of four, and the pole was shortened behind the hind axle. Wheels were generally of lesser diameter than before, about 40 inches for the front, and 50 for the back, with treads of 2½ inches. There was some variation, still, in the track, but the typical waggon was very much a 'broad-gauger'.

The bodies of all these waggons and the undercarriages, for a long time continued to be painted in the traditional way, in spite of a later trend toward simplification. The bodies were Prussian blue with yellow panels on head and tail and the style of lettering and brushwork inherited a fine tradition. The chamfering continued to be of a high standard though the time-factor must already have been looming over everyone concerned. Nevertheless, the work of such wheelwrights as Hardy, of Durweston, Plenty, of Wootton, Forsey, of Symondsbury and Rossiter, of Crewkerne was not to be faulted.

Some of the later waggons, of Dorset, came out of the paint-shops with yellow bodies and red name-panels and the former salmon undercarriages gave place to a vermilion. On yellow panels, the lettering was in black, with red shading, and on red panels, it was in yellow, with black shading. Some of these waggons had their supports made of iron in place of wood.

In Somerset, the last move in waggon design was in the introduction of a shallow barge type, in which the makers dispensed with the former elaboration and the exclusive use of wood for the supports. The body-colour was changed from Prussian blue to indigo, but the undercarriage remained salmon. Lettering on an indigo ground was either white or red, both without shading. The head- and tail-boards were now set between the sides. Such waggons, though distinguishable from other barges, were a break with the past, and were obviously designed to meet the competition with the large firms.

Among the Devonshire wheelwrights, such men as Pike, of Whitestone, west of Exeter; Milford, of Thorverton and Gill, of Exmouth, moved away still further, to produce deeper, plank-bodied waggons which were provided with wooden supports quite distinctive in shape. Even the colour of the body underwent a radical change, from blue to ochre and the heavier appearance of these waggons was emphasised by the fitment of one-piece planks in place of the open out-raves. Cummins, of Bridgwater, eventually moved with the Devon builders but retained indigo for the body, with lettering in white sans-serif. An artificial panelling was produced by lining out in white. One of Cummins' very late waggons was noted near Tewkesbury, in 1965. It had been built for H. W. Biddlecomb, of Prestberries Farm, Hartpury, north of Gloucester.

DORSETSHIRE

Built by Forsey of Symondsbury, Bridport.

Owned by Joseph A. Gibbs, of Moorbath Farm, Symondsbury.

Plate 6

WILTSHIRE AND BERKSHIRE

The three variants of Wiltshire design were all built with straight beds. The first two were made with a full bow, in which the out-raves were continued down to join the hind beam, behind the rear wheels. This bow was set in a transitional curve, which decreased in radius toward the rear. The third design was noted particularly in the Devizes area. It had a body deep enough to clear the hind wheels without a bow-rave. The first and third designs had no middle rave, but the second had. All three had the marked upsweep to the front which was typical of the Wiltshire waggons. The first design was far more numerous than the others and was really the design which one remembers as the Wiltshire.

With these distinctions in mind, the common features may be noted. Along the sides were spaced 10 to 14 flat spars, known as flats, and over the hind-wheel were two wooden supports which were always sloping back. The middle- and hind-standards were always of iron, shaped like a Y and having a stout rope hook, shaped like a pig's-tail. The head-boards were always plain, with a concave top-rail. The tail-boards were also plain but had a double cyma top edge.

The treads of the wheels varied from $2\frac{1}{2}$ to 6 inches, but the majority were $3\frac{1}{2}$ inches or less. They were all well dished, the broad wheels of course more than the narrow, about 10°, and the diameters were about 46 inches for the front and 58 for the back. There were always 10 spokes in the front and 12 in the back.

While the majority had their shafts hinged to the fore-carriage by splinter-bars, a large minority had the simple draught-pin. All carriage hounds were shaped to a very gentle cyma curve to front and back. Braking was by shoe, scotch and tie-chain for the narrow waggons and by tie-chain alone for the broad. Very large ladders were fitted inside the body, fore and aft, to eyes in the floor, to rest at about 60° to the horizontal.

It was almost universal practice to close the space between the top and outraves with boards, called lime-boards. The floor was supported sometimes with four summers, sometimes with two. Nearly every waggon had a Prussian blue body with a red or yellow head-panel, but there were a few with yellow bodies. The undercarriage was red.

The waggon illustrated on Plate 7 shows the second design. It was built for William G. Wadman, of Ogbourne St. Andrew, near Marlborough and was noted in 1948 on a farm at Sydmonton, between Kingsclere and Newbury. The builder's identity was not known, but another and similar waggon, was seen at Kelmscott, near Lechlade. That waggon was painted yellow, in conformity with all waggons north of the Thames.

Among the wheelwrights, there were Barrett of Wroughton, Swindon; Hall Brothers of Grittleton, Malmesbury; Holmes, of Wootton; Hoskin, of Malmesbury; Humphries, of Chippenham and Holly of Pewsham.

The typical Berkshire was, at first sight, easily to be confused with the Oxford, since both had bow-raves and yellow bodies. The wheelwrights who made them are reputed to have endeavoured to improve on the short lock of the Wiltshire and to have been influenced by the merits of the Oxford. For this reason, none was built with a straight-bed, so except for a few which were crooked the typical Berkshire was waisted. There was a clear indication of a transition from Wiltshire to Oxford. The full-bow was retained and very often the closed out-raves, though single or double open-raves were common. A few retained broad wheels but the majority had narrow ones, which were the same size as the Oxford. A curious feature of those built by Gerring, of Milton, near Didcot, was the setting of the butt-ends of the shafts *between* the hounds, instead of outside. There were a few in the west, in Stanford Vale, which had splinter-bars between shafts and hounds. Gerring's waggons, like those built by Day, of Sutton Courtenay, had very well-painted head-boards, with excellent lettering. A further distinction of these last waggons was the orange on the underside of the body and the rave-boards. With the head-panels painted in blue, red, yellow, black and white and a very well-drawn cartouche to enclose the lettering, these waggons were really colourful.

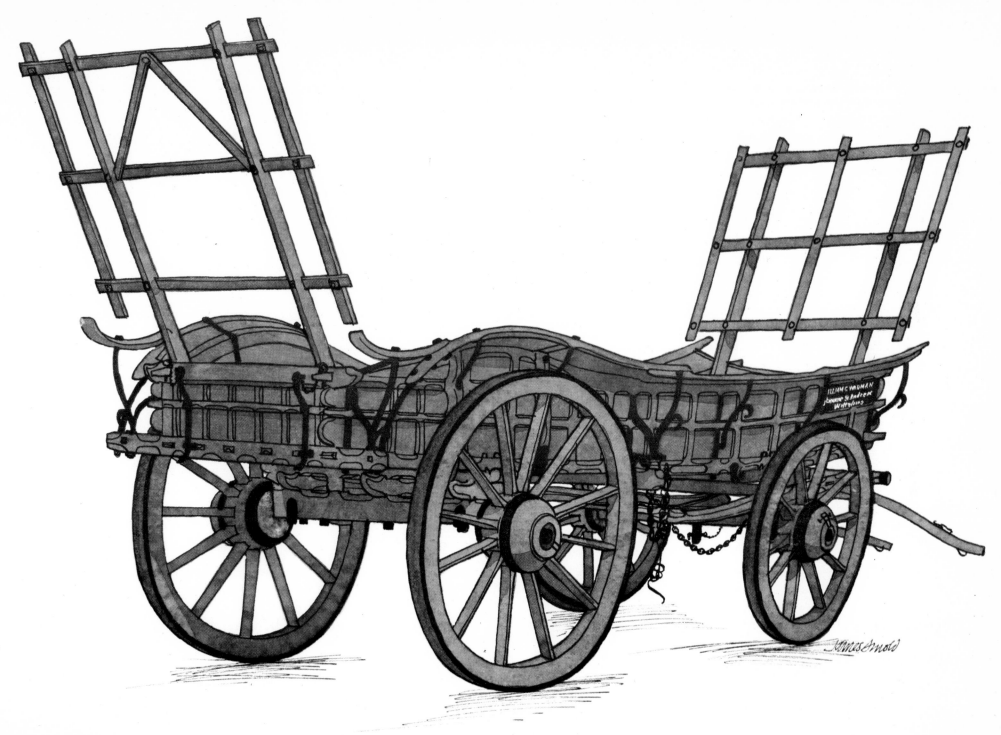

WILTSHIRE

Owned by William G. Wadman, of Ogbourne St. Andrew, near Marlborough.

Plate 7

OXFORDSHIRE

Until the writer took to a bicycle and ventured well beyond the confines of Middlesex and Sussex, 'all waggons were blue'. There was no other colour, so that the first sight of the waggons of Oxfordshire—and Berkshire—provided a shock. Yellow waggons! The impression has remained undimmed. The Oxford was indeed a graceful, almost ship-like waggon which had the hind part of the body arched in a shallow half-bow, to clear the back wheels.

Of all the Oxfords recorded by the writer, just over 97% had this feature to distinguish them from the Berkshires which were nearly all fully-bowed. The second principal difference was the crooked-bed, which 73% of Oxfords had, whereas nearly every Berkshire had a waist-bed. Between these broad distinctions there were the inevitable variants. All the typical Oxfords were yellow, had half-bow raves, a crooked-bed and ran on narrow wheels, but there were some which were blue or brown, or full-bowed, or had waist-beds, but there was never an Oxford which contained *all* these features. Such a waggon would have come from Berkshire.

There were thin, upright spindles along the sides, varying from 13 to 23 in number, and set vertically in the rear half, behind the middle standard, and raking very slightly forward in the front half. Mid-raves were never incorporated in the structure. The standards were always of iron, which was square in section in early designs changing to round in the later, after about 1850. The design of the standards varied, some were V shaped, others H, but in all, the outer iron curved over at the top, where it supported the out-raves. Iron quarter-stays, likewise curved, gave additional support above both wheels.

The head-board was always plain and topped by a robust but finely chamfered concave rail. The tail-boards, however, had spindles, like the sides, often with a middle rail. They were often left unpanelled or with a half-panel and all of them were hinged with 'pin-and-eye' for quick removal. Small ladders were carried fore and aft, the latter at floor-level, but a few in the Northleach and Charlbury area were designed to carry corner-poles. The body was about 12 feet long, sometimes a little more.

With the solitary exception of one broad-wheeler, noted near Evesham, the wheels were invariably narrow, with 2½ inch treads and a dish of about 5°. The diameters were about 48 inches for the front and 60 inches for the back, and with 10 and 12 spokes respectively. No less than 97% had the shafts joined to the fore-carriage by a draught-pin and 68% had only two hounds in the carriage.

Braking was by shoe, tie-chain and a dog-stick, usually, though some were provided with scotches. There were lock-chains from the sides or summers to the fore-carriage bolster. With a tare weight of 18 cwt. the Oxford was probably the lightest of any waggons. The makers must have given a considerable time with the draw-knife and the chamfering indicated that they knew just how far they could safely go. The work was very fine but never overdone.

The body colour was chrome yellow, but occasionally one encountered a blue waggon or even a brown. The undercarriage was vermilion. Lining-out, if present, was slight indeed. The owner's particulars were lettered with little elaboration usually on a yellow panel, but sometimes red, with or without shading. The maker's identity was rarely shown.

Eventually, the Oxford became extremely numerous and was to be found over a vast area, ranging from Cirencester in the west almost to Uxbridge and from the Thames northward to Evesham and a little beyond Banbury. There was a maximum 'density' between Burford, Banbury, Aylesbury and Watlington. There were many wheelwrights, among them were Newport, of Kidlington, near Oxford; Plater, of Haddenham; Lacey, of Naphill, near Princes Risborough; Clanville, of Pyrton, near Watlington; Kench, of Charlbury; Yells, of Maisey Hampton, near Cirencester; Perkins, of Chilworth; Sharp, of Arncott, near Banbury; Baughan, of Ardley; Long, of Aston, near Eastleach; and Walker, of Longwick, near Princes Risborough. Some of Lacey's waggons were short in the body and dispensed with ironwork, all the support being given by wooden members and the raves had a flatter bow. Lacey painted his waggons brown.

Because of the large area of distribution, there was a variety in the names given the Oxford. Some people knew it as a Cotswold, others as a Woodstock, and in Brill, between Oxford and Thame, I heard it called a Cherry-picker, a peculiar name indeed, for which neither my informant nor I could find any explanation. Jenkins, quite reasonably, called the waggon a South Midland, even though the southern part of its distribution lay along the Thames, from its source all the way down to Windsor.

The waggon illustrated on Plate 8 was built by Newport, in 1860 or a little before, for F. M. Kimber, of Church Farm, Hughenden, near High Wycombe. It is representative of the typical Oxford in the general arrangement, although the red head-panel was not commonly encountered.

OXFORDSHIRE

Built c1860 by Newport, of Kidlington, near Oxford.

Owned by F. M. Kimber, of Church Farm, Hughenden, High Wycombe.

Plate 8

SOUTH GLOUCESTERSHIRE

North of Gloucester, and including it, there were a number of fairly individual designs of waggon; between which there was a loose affinity. But south of Gloucester and to the outskirts of Bristol, there was a comparative uniformity between variants of a common design, some of which had a marked affinity with the neighbouring Wiltshire waggons. One might also note the similarity of those of Glamorganshire and wonder who influenced whom. The fully-bowed raves, closed by boards; the pronounced sweep up forwards and the half-moon panel on the head-boards—one or more of these features was present on the Gloucesters.

With or without full-bow raves, the waggons built at Oldbury, Nympsfield, Wotton-under-Edge and Frampton-Cotterell were representative but would have looked equally at home anywhere in North Wiltshire. The real differences were to be found in two features. The first lay in the shape of the wooden supports to the sides, some of which were clamped onto the butt-ends of the cross-beams, instead of standing on the protruding beam-ends. The second was the use of one-piece iron axles on which cast-iron hubs ran. These axles were square in section, sometimes clamped to a wooden bed but usually unsupported. This latter was a comparatively late practice.

The sides were built mostly on straight-beds and were supported either by iron standards or wholly by wood. There were a number of flat or chamfered spars spaced fairly equidistantly along these sides, which were without middle-raves. Generally, the bodies were fairly shallow, but some were deeper than the Wiltshires. This affinity with Wiltshire was emphasised every time the ladders were fitted. They were large, and stood very upright, being set within the body to anchor in the floor-eyes. The out-raves nearly all extended well forward to remind one of a cockroach.

There was some variation in the undercarriages apart from the axles. Some had broad wheels, some had narrow. The broad wheels usually had coned strakes on the front ring and flat hoops on the back, a practice referred to under THE WHEELS. The narrow wheels were usually three to four inches in the tread.

Until recently, a fine waggon stood in the yard of 'The White Hart', at Winchcombe. It was built by Rogers, of Warmley, near Bristol, and until 1963 was owned by Horace E. Taylor, of Netherills Farm, Frampton-on-Severn. It was similar to the waggon illustrated in having cast-iron hubs on straight-through one-piece iron axles. The fully bow-raved body *and* the undercarriage were both painted a deep salmon, and although the wheels had treads of no more than $4\frac{1}{2}$ inches they were shod with two rings of strakes.

Another full-bowed waggon, once the property of James Bishop of Nympsfield, near Nailsworth, was noted as far away as Lower Swell, near Stow-on-the-Wold. It ran on narrow wheels, fairly well dished, and the body had the characteristic fore and aft rake, but the iron standards were fitted to the normally projecting cross-pieces. The body was not straight, but had a crooked bed and was painted yellow on a red under-carriage. The head-board had a 'half-moon' panel painted blue, and the branding, in excellent capitals and a script, was in yellow with black shading.

The waggon illustrated on Plate 9 was built by Thomas Workman, of Wotton-under-Edge. The original owner was not known nor the original colours. The waggon had latterly been in the possession of Chandler Farms, Brailes, Warwickshire and was noted at Great Wolford near Moreton-in-Marsh. It has the typical fore and aft rake of the body, together with the full-bow raves, closed with boards, with the out-raves projecting well forward. The head-board has a half-moon panel, while the tail-board is pure Wiltshire. The extension of the tongue-pole rearward to the hind-beam is characteristic, but of especial interest is the manner in which the hounds and slider are joined—not by a lap-joint but by mortice and tenon, reinforced with long iron strips.

Two features appeared to be common to all waggons, without exception—the brake gear was limited to the tie-chain and no body was divided by middle rails.

SOUTH GLOUCESTERSHIRE

Built by Workman, of Wotton-under-Edge.

Owned by Chandler Farms, Brailes, near Edge Hill, Warwicks.

Plate 9

NORTH GLOUCESTERSHIRE

Within the county of Gloucester there were quite a dozen designs of waggon; some of which were similar, while others differed appreciably. Within the Cotswold Hills, from Stow-on-the-Wold to Cirencester, the Cotswold variant of the Oxford was very common and almost exclusive. Over the rest of the county, the waggons may be grouped into those found to north and south of the City, which until well into the present century had several working wheelwrights.

The northern wheelwrights, working in the area contained by Gloucester, Tewkesbury and the Forest of Dean appear to have been individual men, each producing his own design of waggon. For all the diversity, they were nevertheless 'Gloucestershire' and hardly to be confused with any others. Even the Wiltshireness of many of the waggons of South Gloucester was not present. One was conscious of being cut off from the southern influence by the Severn and the Cotswold Hills.

There was little similarity in the construction of the body, except that none of the designs had bow-raves. Some waggons had straight-beds, some had waist-beds and at least one had a crooked-bed. The systems of body support which were to be noted between Gloucester and Bristol were likewise absent, as all the northern waggons had iron standards fitted to full width of beams which projected beyond the sides. There appears to have been no influence from adjacent counties, nor did these Gloucesters, in turn, exercise much influence on neighbouring counties. It is curious that it was with South Gloucester that Glamorganshire had some affinity. No hybrids were noted on the Herefordshire border, where such might have been expected.

Broad, straked wheels, well dished, appear to have been more common than the narrow ones, which latter were either hoop-tyred or straked. Some of the broad wheels had the back ring flat-hooped. The under frames were of the usual construction and nearly all had the shafts joined by a draught-pin to the fore-carriage hounds. Most waggons had Prussian-blue bodies with salmon or vermilion undercarriages but those built in the Westbury area were buff and those from Tibberton and Tewkesbury were yellow.

Healey, of Gloucester, built crooked-bed waggons, which ran on four-inch hoop-tyred wheels. They were shapely waggons, a little reminiscent of the Sussex, in being fairly deep in the body, with a middle rail and 12 or 13 wood spindles, the sides being supported by cupid's bows of wood, one behind the fore wheel and two above the hind. The main and hind standards were V shaped, and the front edges of the side panels were carved very well. The head-board, set between the sides was painted red and carried the owner's branding. The out-raves were open and the line of the body, between front wheels and tail was straight, with a gentle rise to the front. A curious feature was the flat iron strip in place of the usual wooden front beam. The wheels were slightly dished with 10 spokes in the front and 12 in the back. There were two brakes, a shoe and a tie-chain. Healey gave his waggons a nice distinction by shaping the hounds to a gentle cyma-curve fore and aft of the axle-bed.

A waggon noted near Westbury had a combination of distinctive features. While the broad wheels were straked in the front ring and hooped in the back ring, in the 'Gloucester' manner, this was the only example having closed out-raves and a fore-carriage with splinter-bar. This waggon, by an unknown builder, was the property of Samuel Bullock, of Elton, between Westbury and Cinderford. It had an ochre body, supported by iron V standards and five wooden staves nicely chamfered without elaboration. The treatment of the head-board was notable in having symmetrically carved strips along top and bottom. The branding between was in white letters, shaded red on a blue ground.

The waggon illustrated on Plate 10 is a good example of the work of Teague, of Tibberton, near Newent. It was built for W. R. Fowler, of Tirley. The crooked-bed gave it a good lock, which was helped by the lower sides being turned under at the front end. The broad wheels, being straked *and* hooped, were typical of the county. There was a fair sheer to the body which had double raves. One suspects that Teague may have looked beyond his native parish, further than most were wont, for there is a strong hint of the distant Oxford even though the bow raves were not incorporated.

A waggon noted at Chaceley and belonging at one time to Joseph Spiers was similar to the Tibberton except for a blue body.

NORTH GLOUCESTERSHIRE

Built by Teague, of Tibberton, near Newent.

Owned by W. R. Fowler, of Tirley, near Dymock.

Plate 10

EAST HEREFORDSHIRE

The most commonly encountered waggons had a fairly large body, with plank sides on a straight-bed frame. They were painted either Prussian blue or a peach-buff, both of which had the undercarriages in salmon or red. It was thought that there was some territorial significance especially as other, less common designs were noted in indigo, peacock, ochre and yellow, but the common design was generally distributed irrespective of colour.

Most Herefords had a profile which was of even depth and dead straight between the front wheels and the tail-board, but rising quite markedly forward and they were also conspicuous by their deeply dished broad wheels. In fact the majority of Herefords were broad-wheelers.

The out-raves were nearly always open and set very close to the top-raves, tending to make the waggon appear narrower than it actually was. The plain sides were supported by wooden standards, known by their shape as elbows, at the middle and tail-end. The head-boards were also plain, and topped by arched rails. The similarity between this Hereford and the Shropshire waggons found between Craven Arms and the Severn was sufficiently close that the points of distinction must be set out.

The Shropshire more often ran on narrow wheels. The out-raves were more widely set from the body and were closed, and also they projected as a 'sill' over the head. The sides were supported either by iron standards or wooden ones shaped like a compressed Y and usually called wishbones. There were differences in the colours as follows:

HEREFORD.   Blue bodies had two white grooves
                Buff bodies had two blue grooves
SHROPSHIRE. Blue bodies had three red grooves
                Buff bodies had one to three white grooves
                Yellow bodies had two blue grooves, or more.

There were of course, the inevitable exceptions, e.g. those Herefords, later mentioned, built at Brilley had red grooves on peacock-blue bodies. Most Herefords carried a harvest frame in place of the ladders which all Shropshires carried. These frames, or thripples, were in two parts, to be laid atop the body to overhang all round and meet half-way where they were secured.

The Hereford undercarriages were often works of considerable beauty, with some excellent chamfering on all members. It has been a fascination to run one's fingers over the undulations of this chamfering and to appreciate the hours of work involved. Most waggons had their wheels dished about 12° and from some viewpoints gave the impression of being about to come off their axles. Broad wheels were usually shod with two rings of strakes, but narrower ones, with 5 or 4½ inch treads were 'flat-soled' with a single hoop. A few broad wheels were shod in the Gloucester manner with the inner ring tyred with a flat hoop. The waggon shown on Plate 11 is probably unique in having 6 inch wheels shod with single rings of 6 inch strakes with diagonal joints and flush nails. It was built for Henry Taylor, of Tundridge Farms, near Suckley.

It was in the fore-carriage that the wheelwrights really let themselves go, especially where a splinter-bar was fitted. There were four hounds, the outer being so splayed as to just clear the wheels at the front, and converging to the rear, where they joined the inner ones. The sliders were often duplicated and even the single shafts were reinforced by 'elbows' at their butt-ends. The curves in all these members were complicated enough that only a diligent search in the ash-woods could have produced poles with the suitable natural curves, which, after the most skilful work with the drawknife, were rendered light enough to offset the peculiar structure. Only at the junctions were there any square-sections of wood left.

In the Bromyard-Tenbury district, the waggons were both larger and deeper. The sides were panelled with 12 flat spars, which projected through the side frames, and were divided by a middle rail. The out-raves were supported by 10 wooden stays. The head-board was panelled in a similar manner and a board across the top half carried the branding. The body colour was a Prussian blue. One such waggon was built a little before 1850 for Thomas C. Nott, of Kyre, and is now well cared for by his great grandson, lately of Brockmanton. This waggon had 4½ inch wheels which were 'flat-soled'—i.e. hooped-tyred.

Lock-chains usually ran from a point on the middle beam to the fore-bolster, but on some waggons, found between Hereford and Worcester the chains ran from the rear axle-bed to the fore-bolster, being suspended at three points between to prevent the slack chain from swaying excessively.

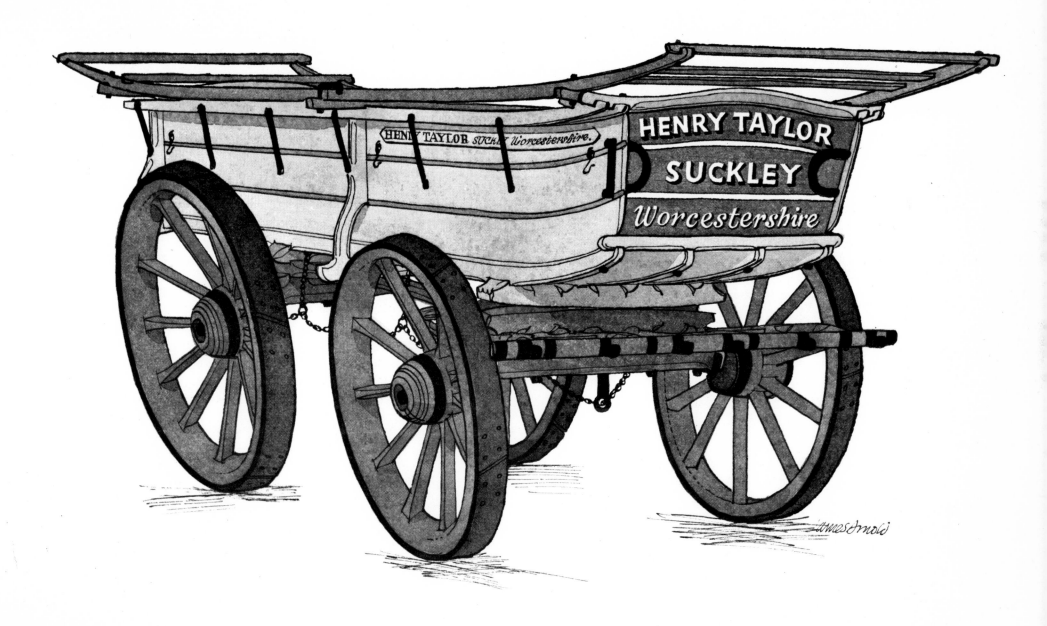

EAST HEREFORDSHIRE

Owned by Henry Taylor, of Tundridge Farm, Suckley, near Bromyard.

Plate 11

WEST HEREFORDSHIRE

The standard design of Hereford waggon was well distributed over the whole county, but in the north and west, along the borders of Shropshire and Radnorshire there were those which could almost be described as variant although they were basically 'native'. Beddoes, of Brilley, between Kington and Hay, produced an elaborately constructed waggon which lacked nothing in the workmanship involved. The sides were divided by mid-raves and were usually well panelled and supported by wood staves of half and full depth in addition to the elbows at the middle and hind beams. Some of these waggons had twin middle standards, or elbows, which met at the foot to form a narrow V. The head-board was treated in a manner similar to the sides and the top rail was arched in the Hereford style. As on every Hereford, the iron stays which held the out-raves were bolted to their outsides and not underneath, a distinctive practice.

In place of either thripples or ladders, these Beddoes waggons were supplied with fenders to sides and head, so accurately made as to appear one piece with the body and every piece of the whole assembly was very finely chamfered. All waggons ran on narrow hoop-tyred wheels and the fore-carriage was designed to take double shafts.

The bodies were painted a blue-green, or peacock, with red grooves in the panel-boards. On the head, a deeply segmented board carried all branding. The owner's name and address, together with that of the builder and the date, all in black with red shading on a white ground with a grey border conforming to the segments.

Plate 12 shows a Beddoes waggon, built in 1900 for James Davies, of Upper Mowley Farm, Titley; and at The Welsh Folk Museum, St. Fagans, Cardiff, they have a similar waggon, built in 1897 for William Meredith, of Fuallt, between Kington and Glascwm. They were the only waggons built west of Severn which were fitted with dog-sticks, for almost without exception the tie-chain alone was fitted for all braking, and it was common practice by most wheelwrights to fit iron cleats to the spokes of rear wheels, at their extremities next the felloes, to take the chafing by the chain.

The Teme valley, above Knighton, divides Radnorshire from Shropshire and below that town soon enters Herefordshire. The waggons of this little district are hybrids of various influences. The plank-sided bodies rise more gently than Herefords but are supported by elbows. At the same time, the out-raves are closed and have a 'sill' projecting over the head-board in the Shropshire style. One such waggon, built for James Preece, of Llanshay Farm, Knighton, conformed to this, and had an ochre body with two blue grooves, as in Herefordshire. The branding was set out in fine white lettering on a long black strip fixed to the fore off-side. Here it may be noted that in nearly every instance west of Severn, this strip was white, with black letters. The Llanshay waggon ran on narrow straked wheels, and the shafts were attached solely by draught-pin to four hounds.

At one time, Merryhill Farm, near Hereford possessed a very fine waggon, once the property of Harry Plant, of Walford, which is near Leintwardine. This waggon had plain sides with a Hereford profile, rising sharply forward. The out-raves and the projecting sill were set widely and closed in the west Shropshire manner, and supported by iron stays all round. The sides were supported by wooden wishbones. The wheels were broad, double straked and very well dished, about 12°. The fore-carriage was in complete conformity with the Clun waggons and many of the Herefords, where splinter-bars and elbows were incorporated. The body was painted yellow, without any grooves and the undercarriage was salmon.

WEST HEREFORDSHIRE

Built 1900 by Beddoes, of Brilley.

Owned by James Davies, of Upper Mowley Farm, Titley.

Plate 12

BRECONSHIRE AND MONMOUTHSHIRE

The penetration of the English waggon into Wales is dealt with at length under GLAMORGANSHIRE. The middle penetration was along the Wye and the Usk, to meet at Brecon and Talgarth. The Wye route came from Hereford, and the Usk from Monmouth and Gloucester. It apparently moved little further beyond Brecon, for central Wales was generally unsuited to the four-wheeler. There are few valleys wide enough to contain the farms on which they can be effectively used.

The waggon shown on Plate 13, was a product of the Talgarth district and had much in common with the Hereford. This waggon was built in 1892, for John Morris, of Pistil Farm, Llanfihangel-tal-y-llyn, near Llangorse and Talgarth. With the waggon was a tumbril of similar vintage and obviously by the same wheelwright. Both had name-boards with similar styles of branding.

The waggon body was blue, without grooves, and the under-carriage was salmon. It had the sharply rising front, from a straight rear end, of the Hereford and presented an odd appearance by reason of the absence of out-raves. It looked happier when the harvest frame was in position. The sides were supported at the tail-end by elbows, but at the middle by straight staves. All wheels, broad or narrow, were fitted with strakes, to prevent skidding on the wet slopes. The style of spoke chamfering was noted on a few Herefords.

It is likely that the waggon did actually penetrate further up the Wye to Builth, where Prothero made some good-looking tumbrils. Father and son were obviously painstaking, for they incised the branding on the head-panel and must therefore have been accustomed users of the wood-carvers tools. One tumbril, built in 1913, for Richard Dyke, of Cwm Celyn, Nantmel, was noted at Weston Beggard, near Hereford.

The very hilly, but nevertheless lowland agriculture of Monmouth-shire called for some use of waggons, and a design did evolve in conse-quence. Bradley, who worked at Llanfihangel-ystern-Llewern, near Monmouth, built straight-bed waggons to run on either broad or narrow wheels. They were not too large for the terrain and were more lightly built than those of Hereford or Gloucester. The sides had no middle raves, but were of medium depth and were panelled with seven to ten spars and supported by iron standards, though some waggons are known to have had wooden standards. The out-raves projected well and were closed by boards. The wheels were fairly dished and were spoked 10 in the front and 12 in the back, and both broad and narrow were straked. Some elements of the hybrid appeared in the 'cow-horn' head-rail of Gloucestershire and the ornamental strip along the head-panel and the style of closed out-raves might have come from the Westbury area.

The City Museum at Gloucester, has a model of a waggon very similar indeed to a Bradley, the original of which was made for D. E. Watkins of Wern-y-Cwm, Llanfetherine, which is not far from Aber-gavenny. At Wolves Newton, between Usk and Chepstow, three genera-tions of Lewis were wheelwrights. All the tools they used are now at St. Fagans. The Monmouthshire waggons were all equipped with ladders, front and back, as necessary. Most of them were blue, but a few were painted yellow.

BRECONSHIRE

Built 1892.

Owned by John Morris, Llanfihangel-tal-y-llyn, Talgarth.

Plate 13

GLAMORGANSHIRE

Wales has always been a country in which various forms of two-wheeled cart and sled have been used exclusively and the penetration of the English waggon has only occurred along certain river valleys. The history of the primitive transport of Wales may be studied in *Agricultural Transport in Wales*, by Jenkins. The gambo proved to be an effective answer to the requirements of hill-farming. It has a low-set platform about 8 feet long by 3 feet 6 inches wide, the side-frames of which are in continuous pieces with the shafts. The wheel diameters are usually a little under 48 inches and narrow of tread. The frames sit immediately on the axle-bed so that the wheels project well above the floor. On each side, next the wheels, a wooden frame called a stile is fitted to keep the load clear of the wheels. It is possible to say to which county a gambo belongs by the manner in which the parts of the stile are arranged. In addition to this variation of bars and uprights, the gambos of at least one county, Brecon, are fitted with removable side boards. All gambos, however have slots in the corners of the platform into which poles can be fitted, in the same way as on the waggons of south-east England, in order to contain the load. In the Teifi Valley, they use a gambo on to which a complete frame can be fitted to occupy the whole length of the platform.

In Central Wales, that is Radnor with the Clun district of Shropshire, some farmers have used a wheel-car. This was substantially built with side frames and sled-nose in one piece about 12 feet or so in length, all underslung below the axle-bed and ran on narrow, straked wheels about 48 inches in diameter. The floor was made of slats, openly spaced, and the fore-end, which projects more than the rear to make it nose-heavy is surrounded by an inclined frame while the rear end is open, but poles may be added to all corners. Stiles similar to the gambo keep the load clear of the wheels. The horse is harnessed in trace to the sled-nosed front and draws the car on its wheels and nose on the level or uphill. In descent the two wheels are locked by tie-chains so that the car goes down in the manner of a sled. One such interesting vehicle, was noted in 1948, at Obley, between Clun and Knighton, and was then in use.

With few exceptions all the gambos and wheel-cars were, and still are, painted salmon. The exception was in the Teifi valley, where a cart, described above, had its upper parts ochre, on a salmon frame.

During the nineteenth century, the English designs of waggon found their way along the coasts of North and South Wales and certain main river valleys. One penetration followed the north coast from Staffordshire. A second came from Shropshire along the Severn, and a third was up the Wye and Usk. The fourth was along the north side of the Bristol Channel into the Vale of Glamorgan where a type of farming was followed to which the four-wheeled waggon was well suited. None of these intrusions was strong enough to proceed very far, but within confined areas, waggons came very much into use.

Taken at first consideration, the typical earlier waggon of Glamorganshire shows in the general arrangement and profile the strongest of influences from South Gloucestershire and even Wiltshire, so much that scarcely an eyebrow would have been raised had one been encountered in those parts.

The Glamorgan was fully bow-raved in the Wiltshire manner with the out-raves at the front projecting well forward. The panelling of the sides together with the mid-rave was again derived, while the head-board had the half moon panel and 'cow-horn' rail of the Gloucesters which were to be seen at Oldbury, Nympsfield and Wotton-under-Edge. The wheelwrights added a bowed rail on top of the 'cow-horn' and filled the space between with a row of turned balusters, repeating this form of adornment on the tail-board. The body had a straight-bed, in conformity with the originals and even the ladders to fore and aft were pure Wiltshire. The builders did not follow the broad wheel trend so all their waggons were narrow wheeled.

It is clear that there was every encouragement to make a handsome waggon, one to be used not only for farming, but for the wedding, the funeral and the Sunday service. The county colours were blue and salmon with the branding in white, shaded black. The iron standards were outstandingly beautiful.

GLAMORGANSHIRE

Owned by Phillip Phillips, Llanishen Fach, near Cardiff.

Plate 14

SHROPSHIRE AND MONTGOMERY

The waggons of Shropshire were of two designs, both of which had straight-bed frames and the body rising sharply forward, with the rear part straight, a characteristic of the Hereford-Shropshire region. The two designs were more or less clearly zoned into East and West, with Craven Arms as the meeting point. The boundary may roughly be drawn from Ludlow up the valley of the Onny where it 'peters out'.

East of the Onny to Bridgnorth, Shrewsbury and a little beyond, the waggons had plain, plank-sided bodies, mostly painted blue and supported by iron standards, though a few had wooden ones. A minority were painted yellow, but were otherwise similar except for 'wishbone' Y standards of wood. Nearly all ran on narrow wheels, many of which were straked. The ladders were set nearly flat on top of the body and the shafts were hinged by either draught-pin or splinter-bar. The under-carriages were not elaborate and were painted red while braking was by tie-chain alone. By comparison with some of the ornate waggons which the reader will have encountered in this book these East Shropshire waggons were markedly restrained.

West of Craven Arms, where tree-clad hills rear majestically on every hand, and where the Romans at last subjugated Caradoc, the contrast in waggon design is indeed breathtaking. When one remembers that one is in the area of wheelcars and where the traveller is often confronted with a succession of 'one in sevens', it is surprising to learn that waggons were used at all. Anyone who knows these hills is not surprised that it was often necessary to use as many as eight horses on a fully laden waggon on those lengthy and arduous gradients between Bishops Castle, Newtown and Knighton. There were usually, in the 30s, a couple of waggons and their teams outside the Anchor, by Clun Forest.

The waggons were comparatively large though not over-deep in the body. They were painted yellow, with two horizontal blue grooves, all round, and the undercarriages were salmon. The sides of the body, on a straight-bed were divided by a single rave and there were a number of upright spars, eight on the sides, plus three iron strips, and four on the head. The whole was supported by wishbone standards with additional supports above each wheel and in front, to support the closed out-raves and projecting sills. A short fore-ladder was supplied.

A few of these waggons ran on narrow wheels, but the majority were broad-wheelers, having a dish of about 12°. The undercarriages were generally similar to those Herefords which had splinter-bars. The outer pair of the hounds converged from a widely splayed front to meet double sliders. Seen in elevation the cyma curve to fore and aft of the axle-bed was conspicuous. The shafts were usually single, with elbow reinforce-ment, like the Herefords, though some had their shafts attached by the simple draught-pin.

The waggon shown on Plate 15 conforms to the above description. It was one of three, built by Francis, of Newcastle on Clun, for Thomas Huffer, who farmed with his two brothers at Fron End, where Offa's Dyke drops down to the river Clun. One of the three waggons always fetched the coal from the station at Broome. The waggon shown had the branding on a yellow board fitted to the side, above the rear bolster, but waggons built by Cadwallader, of Bishops Castle, had this branding on a long black strip on the usual position at the front end of the off side.

One may feel sure that Francis and Cadwallader must have put their heads together to produce unusually beautiful waggons. One of Cad-wallader's waggons may be seen at the Museum of English Rural Life.

The town of Montgomery is very close to Bishops Castle, so we might expect to find that Jones, who built there, was influenced in some degree. Certainly the style of out-rave was present as was the body colour. The standards, however, were not all elbow-shaped, but very often 'wish-boned'. The waggons all ran on narrow wheels nearly always straked, but only slightly dished.

WEST SHROPSHIRE

Clun

Built c1880 by Francis, of Newcastle on Clun.

Owned by Thomas Huffer, Fron End, near Clun.

Plate 15

STAFFORDSHIRE AND DENBIGHSHIRE

In considering the waggons of these counties, we have to consider also the nature of land-usage in the surrounding counties. Cheshire is essentially a county of dairy farming, in which any kind of waggon has had no place. The farms of Derbyshire are all situated on the Pennine where any arable crop is light and where two-wheelers are best suited and adequate. To the east, lies Leicestershire, where the Hermaphrodite design of waggon was in universal favour. The southern part of Staffordshire lies in the industrial area of the Black Country, which for all the brilliance of its canal art, is a void in terms of waggons. To the south-west, one might have expected some stimulus from Shropshire, but again the northern part of that county is partially industrial. To the west of Denbighshire and encompassing a considerable portion of that county lies the mountain region of North Wales. It is therefore to the credit of the wheelwrights of rural Staffordshire and Denbighshire, with Flintshire, that in each county they produced waggons which were strongly individual in design and of sufficient interest that they must be considered separately.

The waggon illustrated on Plate 16 has been completely restored in the workshop at the Museum of English Rural Life and is now resplendent in its original colours of yellow and red. Some of the waggons were built with straight-bed frames, but this example, with an unknown history, but built about 1860, has a crooked-bed, in the Oxford manner, and perhaps a little surprisingly a head-board similar in shape to those waggons built at Cropredy, near Banbury, to which reference is made under NORTHAMPTONSHIRE.

On this crooked frame, the spindle-sided body appears almost straight in profile. The body is divided by a middle rave, below which the front panel-boards follow the curved front half of the frame and turn under at the front to fit the head-board. The iron closing-pins, positioned at the sides of nearly all waggons, are placed in front of the head-panel which is set athwart the sides. In this construction, the Stafford and Cropredy waggons are identical so that one may conjecture whether this was accidental or a matter of one influencing the other. The wooden standards at the middle- and hind-beams are like the Hereford 'elbows' but less emphasised. The out-raves are closed, project well over the sides, and are almost straight in profile. At the front there is a projecting sill, in the West Shropshire manner. Both out-raves and sill are supported by iron stays.

The undercarriage is interesting partly because the wheels are broad, with double straking and deeply dished, about 10°, and also because of the excellence of the chamfering on all members, especially the hounds which are finely ovoid in the rear half. The shafts are attached by the simple draught-pin to the fore-carriage.

The position of the name is the only instance of this arrangement. Although head-board branding is not present, it is likely that some style of this was usual. The tail-board is hinged pin-and-eye, for removal. The brake gear consists of a tie-chain on both sides. Wheel-lock is checked by chains from the side-frames to the bolster. The fitment of corner-poles is unusual for this is almost peculiar to Kent and Sussex. Each pole is passed through a hole in the out-rave-board and rests in a bracket on the side-frame.

The Denbighshire waggon had straight lines everywhere; straight in the bed, the raves, the profile and end elevation. The only relief was in the addition of a bow on the head-rail. The sides were divided by double mid-rave and a panelled effect was created by some 14 flat, bevelled spars. Support was given by wood standards at the middle- and hind-beams with three additional staves on the front and rear halves. Five closing pins were added for increased strength. The summers are concealed, at the front, by the lower part of the head-board. The underside of this board is chamfered to an ornamental edge. The out-raves were well clear of the body and unclosed. They were supported by about 7 curved iron stays.

Unlike the Stafford waggon, the Denbigh ran on narrow wheels and the whole carriage was simpler. A complex pair of shafts was pinned to four hounds.

The colours vary. Of three waggons at The Welsh Folk Museum, St. Fagans, Cardiff, two are red and the third is blue.

STAFFORDSHIRE

Plate 16

ESSEX

The waggons of East Anglia had enough features in common to make it possible to group them into five basic designs, which for convenience may be termed the Large Waggon, the Half-Open, the Bradwell, the Norfolk and the King's Lynn. Of these, the first two were made in variant designs in all three counties, while the last three were strictly regional.

All five designs had the common feature of a very deep waist in which the fore-side pieces turned in sharply to meet the middle beam which was usually of massive proportions. This point in the panel-board was cut away to form the locking-arch which was boxed in on the inside. This locking-arch was in fact to be found on almost every waggon along the East Coast from the Thames to the Humber.

The Large Waggons were common about Haverhill, Halstead and the Hedinghams and bore a superficial resemblance to the Suffolk design. The body was taller at the front than the back and had an emphatic sheer. Some bodies had a single middle rave and some a double and while many had open out-raves, the majority had the typical closed ones. The iron standards were simple straight round or square bars, rising from the middle- and hind-beams to the top-raves. The intermediate wooden staves varied in number, some being straight, others curved. Those waggons with open raves had six or seven iron stays to support them. The head-boards were mostly in two parts, each removable, like the Suffolk, but one waggon, noted at Ridgewell, had a full depth head-board, which was a fixture. The body colours were either blue or green. Like most Large Waggons, the Essex was conspicuous by its large hind wheels, sometimes as much as 69 inches. All were slightly dished. They mostly had 12 spokes in the front and 14 in the back, but some were 10 and 12.

The Half-open Waggon was small by comparison and the peculiar arrangement made it look smaller than it was. Only the lower half of the sides was closed by panel-boards leaving the top half open, and the detachable front-board likewise came only half way, there being no cross-piece to brace the top. A few had intermediate side supports of iron, but the majority had about 6 wooden ones. All of them had straight standards of iron. One waggon, noted at Thaxted had more substantial and buttress-like standards. The fore-ladders rested on the front-board while the hind one rested at floor-level. This design looked somewhat austere and this was more so because chamfering on all members was slight. The body colours were brown, blue or green on red under-carriages.

Wheelwrights between Colchester and Burnham-on-Crouch built their own individual design. It had a fairly shallow body with plank sides which were supported by plain iron standards and intermediate staves, usually of wood but sometimes of iron. The profile presented a moderate sheer with a flat floor. Unlike the Large and the Half-Open waggons this design had a fixed head. The front wheels were set very well forward, making the body appear a little tail-heavy. All of them had hinged tail-boards.

The narrow wheels were but slightly dished and had 12 spokes in the front and 14 in the back. The shafts were attached by a draught-pin to the fore-carriage which was fitted with turn-table rings. All waggons of this design had their bodies painted ochre and the undercarriages red.

The waggon shown on Plate 17 was built by Blank, of Bradwell on Sea, for Messrs. Strutt and Parker, who owned Sandbeach Farm at Bradwell. Aylett, of Southminster also built this design and there were other wheelwrights at Burnham and Layer Marney, near Colchester.

Of all the waggons recorded during the survey in East Anglia, the Half-Open accounted for 41% and the Large for 27% with the remainder collectively accounting for the balance of 32%.

ESSEX

Built by Blank, of Bradwell on Sea.

Owned by Strutt and Parker, Sandbeach, Bradwell on Sea.

Plate 17

SUFFOLK

The Large Waggon was a giant and it was a tall man indeed who could peer over the sides of those built at Hadleigh. This design appears to have originated in Suffolk and to have spread throughout much of East Anglia, in variant forms, to account for some 27% of all waggons recorded in the region.

Three such waggons were noted together at Sampson Hall, near Kersey, one of which is now at the Museum of English Rural Life. I had noted this waggon in 1948 and it was a thrilling reunion to meet an old friend again 20 years later. All were built by Wood, of Hadleigh and had their wheels hung on wooden axle-trees. The sides were supported by straight iron standards and 9 half- and full-depth wooden staves. The panel-boards above and below the middle rave each had two grooves. The head-board was of half-height and made detachable. A wooden cross-piece, likewise detachable, fitted the ends of the top-rails. The height was accentuated by the steep angle at which the closed out-raves projected. One of these waggons is shown on Plate 18.

Scrutton, of Brandeston, built a similar but rather shallower waggon with the two-part removable head-boards, the upper one having an arch top rail and carrying a tip-up seat for the waggoner. It had small front wheels and a three-quarter-lock. The body was blue, with red grooves. Most of the Large Suffolks had massive middle beams.

Another variant of this design was built at Westleton, near Aldeburgh. A few of these had fixed head-boards, but most of them had the familiar detachable ones, in two parts. They were all readily to be distinguished from the other Large waggons, by the carved wooden scrolls and 'motifs' in bas-relief, repeated on both parts of the head. These were always painted in white on a blue body. This design appeared to be confined between Woodbridge and Beccles.

A great many waggons of the Half-Open type were built in Suffolk. Among a number of wheelwrights was Wood, of Stowmarket, possibly a relative of the Wood of Hadleigh. I noted four waggons together, at Ridgewell, belonging to T. Argent, three belonging to Edward Younger, of Walnut Tree Farm, Edwardstowe, and others at Stowupland, Willisham, Finningham and elsewhere. A few of these had wooden axle-trees, and all had the lower half only of the body with panels, leaving the top open. Most had narrow wheels, with 12 spokes in front and 14 in the back though a few were spoked 10 and 12. Several had closed out-raves, which was unusual, but otherwise the open-rave was the rule. Every waggon had the shafts attached to the fore-carriage by a draught-pin. The colours of the bodies were various, blue, green, brown, ochre or peacock—all with red undercarriages.

Two wheelwrights at Long Melford, Silver and Wood, and also Howard, of Layer Marney, were making waggons which were a late departure from the East Anglian tradition. They had a full-lock, with small front wheels, the familiar locking-arch being therefore dispensed with. They had plank-sided bodies with fixed heads and ran on narrow wheels. A number of mass-produced waggons from Yorkshire and Bristol had appeared and one may presume that the waggons made at Melford and Layer were a Suffolk-Essex answer.

Head-board branding and embellishment were little practised by the wheelwrights of East Anglia, except in the King's Lynn district, where the influence from South Lincolnshire was completely dominant. In nearly every instance, the only identity was on the rectangular black plate on the fore off side. The makers were extremely reticent and very few fitted any kind of maker's plate on their products.

The waggons of the region, especially the Large Waggons, were conspicuous by their comparatively large hind wheels, up to 69 inches in diameter. In consequence the smallish fore wheels appeared to be smaller than they were. Throughout the whole region wheels were only slightly dished, and the great majority were spoked 12 and 14 with treads of 3 or 2½ inches, usually hoop-tyred.

Diversity of body-colour was a feature of design. Waggons were recorded as blue, green, ochre, yellow, red, white, brown and orange, with 61% blue and 23% green and 7% ochre and 5% brown.

SUFFOLK

Built by Wood, of Hadleigh, near Ipswich.

Owned by E. W. Wilson and Sons, of Sampson Hall, Kersey.

Plate 18

NORFOLK

The county which was the home of Coke of Holkham and 'Turnip' Townshend, who sponsored the great changes in farming, also produced three designs of waggon, one of which appeared in variant forms.

That design which came to be recognised as the true Norfolk had a shortish body which was usually plank-built, and fairly shallow at the back, rising quite sharply to the front, with a good sheer between. The front wheels were set not more than 15 inches back so that the whole waggon looked tail-heavy. This design incorporated none of the wooden supports which were so conspicuous a feature of the majority of waggons in East Anglia. The head-board was a fixture and indeed, except for the locking arch, this waggon seems no more than a distant relative of the design found in South-east Essex.

All these Norfolks were painted blue, and had closed out-raves supported by iron standards and about 5 iron stays. There was some fine chamfering on the front end edge of the body-sides and the top and bottom rails of the head were similarly treated. Some had turn-table rings fitted to the fore-carriages but retained the tongue-pole. Wheel treads were narrow at $2\frac{1}{2}$ inches and the dish was slight. There were usually 12 spokes in the front and 14 in the back, but one waggon recorded had this order reversed. Among a number of known wrights were Crane, of Dereham and Fransham, and Cresswell, of Narborough who built the waggon shown on Plate 19 for H. Birbeck, of West Acre, near Swaffham.

At Great Massingham, I chanced upon a variant of the Norfolk. The sides of this waggon were shallow enough to require a half-bow rave in order to clear the large hind wheels which were equally spoked with 12, front and back. In all other features, the general arrangement, the profile and forward set of the front wheels, this waggon was in conformity except that over the hind axle there were two wooden staves to support the sides. Unfortunately, there was no identity of maker or owner.

The Large East Anglian waggons were to be found in the centre of the county, between Diss and Fakenham and were made at Wymondham, Melton, Palgrave and elsewhere and were hardly distinguishable from the Suffolks. One becomes accustomed to finding waggons many miles from their 'native heath' but I was astonished to find a Large Waggon at Michaelchurch Escley, where Herefordshire encloses a large slice of the Black Mountains. This was once the property of Bilham Woods, of Lodge Farm, North Lopham, near Diss. And just to keep it company, there was a Half-Open Waggon built by Smith, of Morley, near Wymondham. Two waggons less suited to the mountain foot-hill type of farm one could not imagine for this was more the home of sleds and gambos.

The Half-Open referred to was a representative of the Norfolk variant of this design and one a little different from those found in Suffolk and Essex. It had a straight planked body, without locking-arches as the front wheels were quite small. The fore-carriage had a turn-table ring. The wheels had $2\frac{1}{2}$ inch treads and 10 spokes in the front and 12 in the back. The open top half was supported by iron standard and stays. The entire waggon was painted red, with a blue groove along the side planks. This type was also built by Crane but the wheels had the spokes 12 and 14 and the body colour was blue.

To the west of Swaffham, the district about King's Lynn is really an extension of South Lincolnshire, in terms of waggon design. Waggons built by Bolton, of King's Lynn all more or less followed the Holland tradition. The probable explanation was that this area belonged less to the Norfolk cornlands than to the farming about the Wash.

These waggons were quite large and deep in the body, and most had double mid-raves and about 20 spindles. The head-boards were never removable, always fixed and all the proportions followed those of the East Midland design. The massive framework of the Large East Anglian was dispensed with and in fact, only the locking-arch was retained. The change-over was completed by the colour scheme, which was wholly orange with extensive lining-out in black. Many waggons had the wood standards of Northampton but a few had iron standards and stays and also a single middle-rave.

There were three together at Rising Lodge, near Lynn, belonging to J. Ruane and Sons, who also owned a number of very fine Scotch carts, made by Bingham, of Long Sutton. H. Folley, of Lutton, near Holbeach, at one time owned both a waggon of this design and also a 'true' Norfolk.

NORFOLK

Built by Cresswell, of Narborough, near Swaffham.

Owned by H. Birbeck, Castle Acre, near Swaffham.

Plate 19

SOUTH LINCOLNSHIRE—HOLLAND

As a note of interest—The Parts of Lincolnshire are similar to the Ridings of Yorkshire.

Throughout the three Parts of Lincolnshire, there were two main designs of waggon, one of which was common to both Kesteven and Lindsey and the second, which was exclusive to Holland. Except that both designs incorporated the locking-arch common to nearly every waggon built between the Thames and the Humber, there were no features which were common to both. This sharp division between the adjoining parts of Holland and Kesteven is a matter of interest and conjecture. In other regions one finds in a number of cases, that one design will be common to two or more types of terrain and farming, and even several designs being found on one terrain. But there is no apparent reason for the break between Holland and Kesteven. The latter design appears to be a survival of a much older one.

The Holland waggons conformed to a basic design which appears to have been centred on Stamford, spreading to Boston and King's Lynn as an orange waggon with a locking-arch, to Rutland in one direction and to Huntingdon in the other, as a brick-red waggon with the locking-arch, and nearly all the way to Banbury as an orange waggon, without the arch. The Large Cambridge was also in conformity and its alternative colours of either blue or ochre could not conceal this.

The Hollands were found in three variant forms. One retained the locking-arch and the second, having a crooked-bed, dispensed with the arch. Both had two middle-raves and about 23 spindles along the side. The third form retained the arch, but had only one middle-rave and 8 or 10 spars and in place of the usual two summers, it had four.

All three variants were large, deep-bodied waggons with a fine standard of finish. The chamfering was in the high tradition of the East Midland region. Likewise the lining-out on nearly all members or the orange body and undercarriage together with the style of branding on the head-boards made these waggons conspicuous components of the landscape about the Wash. The head-boards carried formal ribbon-work and floral scrolls which contained particulars of the owner and, on some waggons, the builder and date as well. Some waggons had the latter similarly displayed on the tail-board. The owners took great pride in the maintenance of their waggons and carts, and it was unthinkable to allow any on the road in other than first-class order.

The wheels were mostly narrow, not more than 4 inch, both front and back of good size, and moderately dished. It was usual to have 12 spokes in the front and 14 in the back and it was also usual to have the shafts joined by a splinter-bar to the fore-carriage.

The waggon shown on Plate 20 was built by Bingham, of Long Sutton in 1896, for J. T. and A. H. Piccaver, also of Long Sutton. This waggon was oil-lubricated and has the axle-caps which were always fitted to such waggons. Ladders were not supplied, but deep upright fenders, or 'high-raves' were fitted all round. These waggons were used principally for transporting the potato crop from the farms to the stations.

In its variant forms, all resplendent in orange for both the body and the undercarriage, this design was produced by many wrights between King's Lynn and Boston, all catering for farmers exacting in their requirement and who kept everything immaculate. The waggons were made in two sizes, to carry 3 and 5 tons of potatoes in 1 cwt. bags, and each was equipped with a short step-ladder. At other times, sheep and pigs were also carried, when the 'high-raves' were fitted. Many of the waggons were fitted, to specification, with oil-lubricated axles, with the tell-tale caps which screwed on. Some farmers, however, preferred the older greased axle, because some of their men were apt to cross the threads in replacing the caps.

It should be mentioned that tumbrils, known locally as Scotch carts, were made in very large numbers, with either fixed or drop sides for easy loading. That this was an area of large farms is indicated by the fact that two brothers, between them, owned nearly 40 carts and 10 waggons, all numbered. Wheelwrights in addition to Bingham, were Bolton of King's Lynn; Walton, of Long Sutton; Goddard, of Sutton Bridge; the Robinson brothers, and Green, both of Whaplode; Taylor, of Spalding; and Chappell and Bishop, both of Deeping St. Nicholas.

SOUTH LINCOLNSHIRE

Built 1896 by Bingham, of Long Sutton, near Holbeach.

Owned by J. T. and A. H. Piccaver, of Long Sutton.

Plate 20

NORTHAMPTONSHIRE

In the region comprising the counties of Northampton, Rutland, Huntingdon, the Holland Part of Lincolnshire, the King's Lynn district and northernmost Buckingham, the wheelwrights seem to have been infused with a common ideal which penetrated into Cambridge. Whether the waggons were painted orange, brick-red or blue was incidental, however traditional those colours were. Basically, there were two designs or variants, one with the locking-arch and the second with a straight-bed. These features apart, all the waggons were big, with deep bodies, nearly all of which had two middle raves and only a slight sheer. All the wheelwrights concerned seemed imbued with a tradition of brilliant colour and ornament.

The Northamptons were built to a straight-bed and had the typical box-like deep body of the region. The locking-arch was never adopted anywhere south-west of Stamford. These waggons had a gentle sheer which rose slightly more to rear than forward. The sides were divided by two middle raves and there were 16 to 20 spindles along each side. The middle- and hind-standards were always of wood, with two additional staves over each wheel. Some of the waggons, built at Flore, in the southern half, had twin middle-standards, each on its own beam, the hindmost being slightly the smaller. Every waggon had the out-raves closed except where the tails of the front ladder fitted. The head-boards were set athwart the sides and their top rails were gently arched. It seemed that whereas in Wessex, they put the load *on* the body and between tall ladders, in the East Midlands they put as much as possible *in* the body, and designed accordingly.

The construction of the fore-carriage and shafts was often quite elaborate, with the hinge by either draught-pin or splinter-bar. In the southern half of the county the wheels had 10 spokes in the front and 12 in the back, but the northern wrights followed Holland with 12 and 14 respectively. Apart from this difference, all wheels were dished about 5° and had hoop-tyres of 3 to 4 inch tread. Braking was by shoe, scotch and tie-chain.

A very fine waggon was noted at Benefield, near Oundle. Phoebe Osbond, the owner, told me, in 1948, that the waggon was built some-time before 1850, as a road-carrier, to work between Oundle and London—the advent of the railways suggests that in fact it was little used as such and shortly went on to farm work. This waggon was last painted by Stubbs, of Wakerley, in the Welland valley, west of Stamford. The axle-caps, incised Matthews, another wheelwright, indicated lubrication by oil so that the undercarriage was of much later date than the body, possibly 1890. The waggon is shown on Plate 21 and it can be said that the quality of the painting on the head-board followed the long tradition of the region, with no sign of any decline.

Philips, who worked until recently, at Flore, near Weedon, did not follow the Stamford design of panel decoration, but produced his own, of equal merit. In this, the name was set across the full width in bold sans-serif letters, with the farm and county below, flanked by formalised sheaves of wheat. Everything was rendered in first-class lettering in white, shaded black and black, shaded white on the orange ground. The Flore waggons usually had the builder's name, address and date *incised* along the foot. There was no hiding under the bushel in Northants and the head-boards were the crown to a brilliant conception.

The town of Banbury, situated at the crossing of several ancient ways, including the 'Jurassic Way' or more commonly, Banbury Lane, was also the meeting point on the 'Waggon-Map', of the ship-like bow-waggons of the Cotswolds and Wessex and the box-waggons of the East Midlands and beyond. So it was, perhaps, inevitable that one wheel-wright should produce the hybrid which cushioned the meeting. Sumner, of Cropredy, just north of Banbury, built a straight-bed waggon, similar to the Flore, but shallower so that the open-raves just cleared the hind wheels. The front end was turned under, below the single mid-rave. Sumner used wooden standards with intermediate iron stays to support the raves. The head-board was set athwart the sides, similar to Stafford practice—a long-distance influence perhaps, but in which direction? The bodies were painted the same yellow as the nearby Oxfords and the undercarriage was likewise 'Oxford' in arrangement, and painted red.

The lettering on the head-board was always done well, in sans-serif, and black-letter. A few of these waggons were recorded further afield than the 'home area'. One at Condicote, near Stow-on-the-Wold, two at Casey Compton, near Northleach and another at Streatley-on-Thames.

NORTHAMPTONSHIRE

Built c1850 and repainted by Stubbs, of Wakerley, near Stamford.

Owned by Phoebe Osbond, of Benefield, near Oundle.

Plate 21

CAMBRIDGESHIRE

This county, tall and narrow on the map and extending from Wisbech in the north almost down to Royston, contains both Hereward's Fenland and the gentle hills which meet Lamb's Hertfordshire. In regard to waggons, it is bounded on the east by various designs of East Anglia and on the west by the variants of the East Midlands. One may well wonder what to expect of the county's wheelwrights.

They evolved two designs each of which was influenced, one by the East Midlands box-waggon and the other by the East Anglian Half-Open. The two were in such striking contrast that it seems impossible for them to have been built in the same small area. But there are tell-tale features which put this beyond doubt. The locking-arch of East Anglia was apparently not acceptable, so the wheelwrights shaped the side frames with a hump like a canal bridge where the front wheels meet the sides. This curious hump can be seen in the Great Road Waggon, now at the Museum of English Rural Life, and it was perpetuated in a number of Cambridge waggons, especially the Half-Open type. This hump was not universal however, and some of the late descendants of the Road Waggon had beds which were straight except for a waisting on the outside edges.

The Great Road Waggon looked like an East Midland in general arrangement though more heavily built, but it was painted blue and red. The deep sides were divided by two middle raves and there were 20 spindles all vertically arranged along the sides. There were twin middle standards each on its own beam, with a single standard at the back. Surprisingly these were of iron shaped with deep cupid's bows where they met the raves. The open out-raves were supported by 9 iron stays, of which the second, on the near side, carried the waggoner's flask. Over the front wheel there was an additional wooden support. The head-board was not flat but slightly bowed and in two parts in the Suffolk manner. The lower part was a fixture and repeats the 'rail and spindle' of the sides. On this, a red board carried the identity 'Webb, West Wickham, Cambs'. There was a wooden bas-relief disc, painted red, underneath. The top part was removable.

For a waggon of its size, the wheels were not over-large, being 45½ and 62½ inches respectively, with treads of 4 inches in front and 3½ at the back—curious this. This waggon is stated to have been built at Horseheath in 1780 and to have worked as a carrier between Streetly End and London. A study of the O.S. 1 inch map No. 184, shows Horseheath on the A604, 4 miles west of Haverhill, with Streetly End consisting of no more than a windmill, an inn and several cottages. West Wickham lies just to the north. Wherever this waggon started from or went to, its principal interest lies in the predominantly Midland influence in a design produced so close to villages which were East Anglian in everything. In this bit of England, not far from the Gog and Magog Hills, one can pass in and out of Cambridge, Essex and Suffolk in a matter of minutes.

At Ickleton, between Cambridge and Saffron Walden, but much nearer the latter, Godfrey made some fine waggons which were clearly descendants of the Road Waggon. One of his waggons was recorded at Wenden Hall, which was then farmed by Henry Duke. He was the kind of man, graceful and cultured, who one would associate more with letters than the plough. His farm was in Wendens Ambo, near Saffron Walden.

Except for the straight-bed and wooden supports, his waggon was a smaller version of the 1780 waggon, even to the bow front. The fore-carriage was designed to take double shafts and the tongue-pole extended to the hind-beam. The twin standards were similar to those on the Flore waggons of Northants. A second waggon of this design belonging to James Welch, was recorded at Ickleton, with a brown body.

Henry Duke also owned two of the Half-Open Waggons. They varied in the general arrangement of components but were hump-sided as described above. Both had their upper sides without panelling, and had half-height, detachable head-boards on which the fore-ladder rested. The sides of both had 20-21 spindles, which the East Anglians did not have. One design had cranked iron standards and the second had straight ones. The first had two wooden supports over each wheel, while the second had one. One had the tongue-pole extending to the hind-beam. Both had tail-ladders at floor-level.

CAMBRIDGESHIRE

Built by Godfrey, of Ickleton, near Saffron Walden.

Owned by Henry Duke, Wenden Hall, Wendens Ambo, near Saffron Walden.

Plate 22

NORTH LINCOLNSHIRE

The waggons which had always been built in the Parts of Kesteven and Lindsey, differed in every respect, not only from Holland, but from every other region in England, and must therefore be considered separately. Their profile, sheer and general appearance, however they were viewed, did suggest a closer kinship with some of the Dutch waggons, especially the 'Sunday Car' in which the farmer and his family once drove to Service.

The absence of out-raves made the body appear narrower than it was, when viewed from front or back. Where most waggons had head-boards which were much wider than tall, the North Lincolns had boards much nearer the square so that the narrowness was further accentuated.

Some waggons had single middle rails while others had double, and it is likely that one could identify the builder by this, apart from the branding. All of them had about 25 spindles each side, raking progressively from the middle standard. The sides were supported solely by iron standards at the middle- and hind-beams and as there were no out-raves to be supported, this was the only ironwork. In place of the raves, large fenders were dropped into brackets provided. There were two a side and one each at front and back, to deepen the body by some nine inches. Some builders supplied harvest frames, in addition to fenders. These frames were somewhat like those fitted to Hereford waggons.

The frame was turned in sharply behind the front axle to permit a good lock and to this end, the front wheels were set well forward. The locking-arch was in fact the solitary feature to associate this waggon with the East Coast. The single summer in the frame was quite large, about six inches wide and projected to present a beautifully chamfered nose. The undercarriage was simple, with two hounds without any reinforcement, in the fore-carriage. The bolsters and pillow were quite shallow. The shafts, however, were complexly arranged and draught-pinned directly to the hounds, which projected very shortly in front of the axle-bed. Some builders fitted four hounds rather than two.

The large wheels were moderately dished with treads of 3 inches. The diameters were about 50 inches in front and 60 in the back, while the number of spokes were either 10 and 12 or 12 and 14. The retention of wooden axle-trees in many of these waggons is of interest. To the north we find this practice in Yorkshire while to the south, in Holland and all around Stamford, the oil axle-arm was much in favour. It would seem that Kesteven just turned its back on Holland.

Waggons built by Wright, at Alvingham, near Louth and by an unknown wright at Leadenham, between Newark and Sleaford, had stoutly panelled head-boards, the arrangement of which can be seen in the illustration on Plate 23. This waggon was built for John S. Reeve of Leadenham, in 1829. The colour as restored at the Museum of English Rural Life, is an indigo on a red undercarriage. The branding and the scrolls are in white, shaded Cambridge blue. Wright of Alvingham and his father and grandfather before, finished their waggons a little differently. The owner's name was lettered on a long white panel on the head rail, and the village and county were in two white discs in the top corners of the panelling, and quite properly, the maker's name centrally at the foot. A Wright waggon may be seen at the Museum of Lincolnshire Life. Another waggon, built by Rowe, in 1848, for John Stubbs, was restored by Dobbs, of Covenham, in 1962 for Sir Geoffrey Harmsworth, of Tealby. This was all-over orange as is a Newark waggon now in the collection owned by R. Gilbey of Ugley Green, Essex.

Both Rainforth and Cooke made waggons radically different from Kesteven-Lindsey, in the City of Lincoln. Except for the retention of the locking-arch, these resembled nothing produced on the East Coast, except the Barge waggons. These waggons, similar to each other but not identical, were robustly constructed and the arch permitted larger front wheels than was possible on the Barge. The bodies were plank-sided and well supported with quite stout iron standards. The head-boards and the tails were likewise of heavy planks. The colours varied, one built by Rainforth which was noted at Bingham's yard, at Long Sutton, was maroon all over with bold panel lining in black. This waggon had oil-lubricated axles. Another, built by Cooke in 1900, for John England had had the village name blacked out as a precaution during the war. The lettering on the head had been executed with a fine taste and skill. All the space around it had been filled with scrolls and flourishes which were both original and above criticism.

NORTH LINCOLNSHIRE

Built in 1829, at Leadenham, near Sleaford.

Owned by John S. Reeve, Leadenham House.

Plate 23

YORKSHIRE

A study of an Ordnance Survey map which indicates the land usage of the three Ridings, will show that the largest county contains a comparatively small area in which corn is grown. It is confined mainly to three areas; the foothills and the valleys surrounding Whitby and Pickering; the area between York and the coast, including the Wolds and Holderness; and the little of the West Riding not engulfed by heavy industry. West of Harrogate and Thirsk the country shortly ascends to the Pennine moorland, where sheep in their tens of thousands graze in their lonely silent world. We next have to remember that these areas of cornland are at the northernmost extremity of the Waggon Zone of England and Wales. Beyond this limit there were no waggons made or in use. The very nature of the terrain and the type of farming precludes the use of transport other than light carts and sleds, of which a number of types of each were extensively used. We have to return to the lower farms for evidence of waggons.

The Yorkshire waggons of the three areas had sufficient in common in detail and arrangement that they were mostly to be distinguished by size. Except for those used on the Wolds and in Holderness, they were generally shorter in the body than most, and their appearance had a practical forthrightness that one might expect there. The largest were as much as four feet longer than the shortest and were much used on the farms between York, Flamborough Head and the Humber. Some of those used in Holderness were fitted with broad, straked wheels, which gave especial interest to this corner of Yorkshire, near Kingston-upon-Hull, because over the county as a whole, there was the paradox of narrow, hoop-tyred wheels on wooden axle-trees. They were to be found on nearly every waggon made, down to the last quarter of the nineteenth century. All these waggons, narrow or broad, had straight-bed bodies, with front wheels of small enough diameter that they could turn under the body. No insection was needed and but for the retention of the tongue-pole, all these waggons would have been fully-locking. However, there was always the danger of such a waggon turning right over when being manœuvred on uneven hilly ground.

All these designs had plank-sided bodies which were supported by iron standards alone. The out-raves were made of single wide planks and the comparative simplicity and absence of decoration indicates that practical considerations overruled all else. Some element of decoration was not entirely absent, for most bodies had several grooves equidistant along the sides, which were always painted in a colour which contrasted with that of the body. The framework of the head was often very well panelled and chamfered, in fact some waggons had quite complicated arrangements of spindles and rails, in sharp contrast to the austere appearance of the sides. Where such head-panelling was adopted, the arrangement was repeated in the tail-board.

At one time, many waggons had the fore-carriage designed to enable a centre draught-pole to be fitted as an alternative to the normal shafts. Two, three or four horses were harnessed to the pole while whipple-trees were attached to the outer ends of the carriage, much in the manner adopted on pair-horse-drawn brewers' drays. On many of the later waggons, the shafts were attached by either draught-pin or splinter-bar.

Some of the early waggons used on the West Riding farms bore much more resemblance to those of the distant East Midlands, differing mainly in having removable head-boards. The bodies were deep enough to justify the incorporation of double middle raves and the sides were supported mid-way by narrow V-shaped standards of wood. The usual additional supports, also of wood, were positioned over each wheel. These were shod with four inch tyres. A model of this design may be seen in the Castle Museum at York.

The waggon shown on Plate 24, is representative of a fairly late design, built by Pearson of Egton, near Whitby, for W. Jackson, of Roxby, near Staithes. It had the characteristic wooden arms and ran on narrow, hooped wheels. The choice of maroon, for both body and carriage was a change from the inevitable blue.

At Beverley, Crosskill established such a reputation for his mass-produced waggons that they became common in many regions of England and Wales, partially because the basic designs could be superficially modified to conform to the county designs. They were nearly all three-quarter lock, and the wheels were built on cast-iron hubs.

YORKSHIRE

Built by Pearson, of Egton, near Whitby, N.R.

Owned by W. Jackson, of Roxby, near Staithes.

Plate 24

ACKNOWLEDGMENTS

In this realisation of a long-standing ambition, I have the pleasure of acknowledging gratefully the advice and assistance in many forms from the following sources, all of which have proved indispensable. J. P. Bingham, Bexhill, Sussex. G. W. Casbon, Barley, Herts. W. H. J. Drew, Frampton Cotterell, Gloucester. F. Heathfield and Son, Ashford, Kent. O. Johnson, Gorsley-Linton, Herefords. L. W. Philips, Flore, Northants. A. Preston and Son, Cradley, Herefords. F. Sumner, Cropredy, Oxon. G. Weller, Sompting, Sussex. N. Wheeler, Clee St. Margaret, Salop, and the thousand and one farmers who opened their gates to me. I have an especial word of thanks to C. A. Jewell, B.Sc., Keeper of the Museum of English Rural Life, Reading University, for allowing me the fullest access to the Library there, and no less to R. A. Salaman, Harpenden, Herts, for engaging in considerable correspondence. And finally to my publisher for venturing where others, of lesser perception, refused.

ROSEDALE
LOWER EGLETON
LEDBURY
HEREFORDSHIRE

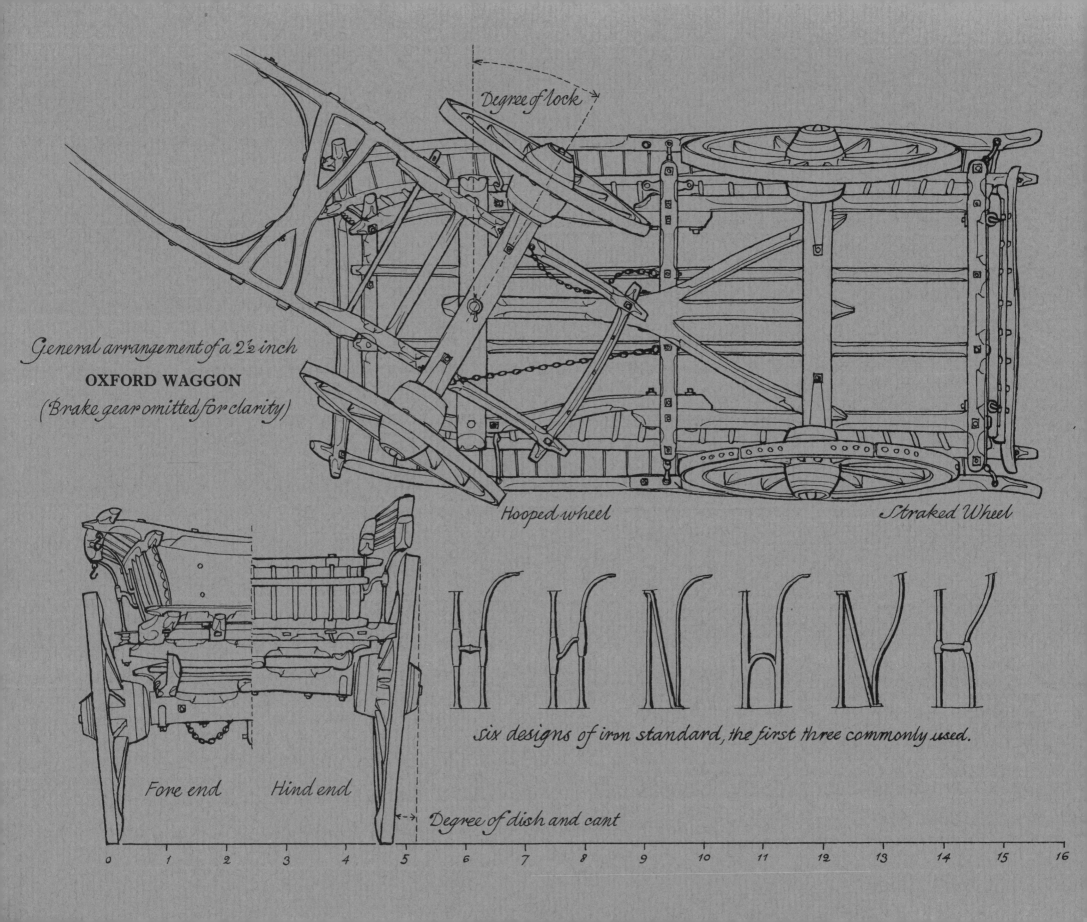

Degree of lock

General arrangement of a 2½ inch

OXFORD WAGGON

(Brake gear omitted for clarity)

Hooped wheel

Straked Wheel

Fore end   *Hind end*

Degree of dish and cant

Six designs of iron standard, the first three commonly used.

0   1   2   3   4   5   6   7   8   9   10   11   12   13   14   15   16